Praise for Chip Helm and this information-packed, practical, and essential book about sales...

"Chip Helm is relatively unique as a visiting instructor in the college classroom. He is both inspirational and instructive as it relates to the sales profession. He has always been met with considerable student enthusiasm over the last few years in my classes."

—**Dick Canada**, Founder for the Center for Global Sales Leadership and Marketing Professor, Kelley School of Business, Indiana University, Bloomington, IN

"Each semester I have the good fortune to have Chip Helm talk to my undergraduate and MBA students. Chip brings over 30 years of sales and sales management experience into the classroom. Whether Chip talks about "Branding Yourself" or his "Five Steps to Sales Success," the students come away with intuitive and actionable insights into selling themselves or a product. Chip's high-energy presentations are contagious as he captivates his audience with humor and outstanding sales knowledge."

—**Ramon A. Avila**, George and Frances Ball Distinguished Professor of Marketing, Ball State University, Muncie, IN

"Chip Helm is someone who has a strong emotional empathy that resonates with everyone. He has generously given his personal time to speak at collegiate sales club meetings and has shared his story and experiences from working at Cook Medical for 32 years. He encourages others to succeed and strongly believes that each individual will find their own unique way to accomplish great things in life."

—**Maddie DuBois**, President of Sales Club at Kelley School of Business

"Thanks Chip! Appreciate all the direction and mentorship you have given me over the last eight years. I've said it before, I'll never stop calling you for suggestions and help throughout my career."

—**Greg Toplitz,** Manager, HCP Education and Development, Medical Education (Americas), *Cook Medical*

"Chip Helm is as passionate about sales as anyone I've ever met. With an extensive and impressive history in his time at Cook Medical, Chip Helm embodies the ideal, personable salesman. As a sophomore in the Kelley School of Business, I am constantly looking to further develop my professional sales skills. With Chip's aid and mentorship, he has provided me a glimpse of what it is like to be a professional in the world of sales, and I am glad to have a relationship with him."

—**Adam Scheck**, student, IU Kelley School of Business – 2020, Marketing & Professional Sales Major

"It's always a grand day when you come to Kelley to guest lecture – seriously! We are so appreciative of your insight and "real world" perspective in the classroom as well as when you participate in various other sales activities. The center's corporate partners are critical to our success, and your role is instrumental in supporting our sales mission. We could not exist without Cook's generosity and belief in what we do, and we are so grateful for your positive energy, time, and support."

—**Sonya Dunigan,** Assistant Director, Center for Global Sales Leadership, Indiana University, Kelley School of Business

"My experience with Chip Helm was hearing him give a talk to one of my college classes during my junior year. The class discussed consultative selling, and Chip's insight was crucial. He creates little ounces of wisdom called "Chipisms" which are off-the-cuff bits of insight into both selling and life. Some mentioned during my class period were, "We're all in sales;" "You need a goal, and your goal can change;" "You have to decide what you want to do in life;" "Use what you've got to your advantage." The most impactful "Chipism" to me was, "You need a goal, and your goal can change." Previously in my life, I tended to shy away from specific goals, and rather just do the best I can because I didn't want to fail reaching my goal. This message inspired me to not view goals as scary or unreachable, but rather my accomplice in becoming a better person, and achieving what I want in my life."

"He also outlines the *5 Truths of a Sale* which are 'Follow up;' 'Never give up on a customer;' 'Relationships;' 'Networking;' and 'Passion.' If you have these five components on the forefront in your mind when approaching a sale, you will ultimately find success. Maybe not the first time, but with persistence and hard work, you will eventually create a successful selling environment."

—**Erin Weber**, Student, Center for Global Sales Leadership
Kelly School of Business

"Chip is a fantastic source for college students, recent graduates, and others new to the world of sales. He combines a sincere desire to help and inform with a quick wit, dry sense of humor, and real-world talk to combine into someone who is repeatedly asked for and requested to speak at collegiate employer panels across Indiana. Chip is someone who will willingly stay after and speak to as many students individually as needed, get the entire audience laughing at a story, or be blunt and tell them honest to goodness truth about expectations out in the 'real world.' When Chip is talking, all eyes are riveted and barely a blink happens. He is a fantastic partner to Indiana State University and our students are better due to his continued presence working with them.

—**Kyle Harris, M.S., CDF**, Assistant Director, Career Center,
Liaison to Bayh College of Education,
Liaison to Scott College of Business, Indiana State University

"Humility is a word that most people do not associate with career professionals and salespeople. But that is exactly what struck me about the book by Chip Helm, where he unequivocally bats for humility as a key character requisite for people to succeed in their careers. His conviction that humility can help professionals improve their work-life balance is a very engaging and interesting concept, one that professionals forget sometimes."

"I thought the talk about Personal Branding was eye-opening. I know that I need to watch what I post on social media, but it was a different twist when I actually thought what my personal brand was. The tip you gave about asking other people what they thought of me was something I never thought of before. It was shocking/refreshing hearing about your struggles in the business world. Everyone normally talks about the success they had, but never touch on the hard times in their lives. I loved the energy and enthusiasm so early in the morning. You really did a good job including everyone in the conversation. I think it is a good idea having people use name tags because you got people to volunteer speaking who normally would not talk. I am very interested in reading your new book."

—**Shannon Eden,** Student,
Ball State University

"Recently, I had Chip Helm come and share his thoughts on the concepts of personal branding and his take on the '5 Truths of Sales.' Not only did the students enjoy his presentation, they actually ended up getting a lot of useful tips/tricks about how they could build and maintain their personal brands, while being successful in sales. I am really looking forward to having Chip back in front of my students in the next semester."

—**Deva Rangarajan, Ph.D.** Associate Professor of Marketing,
Associate Director of the Center for Professional Selling,
Miller College of Business

"Through thick and thin, you have been my leader and our team leader as RM group for long time. We were all and always united in support as our team. You have been and always will be an outstanding mentor and leader for us and selfishly for myself in particular."

—**Brent Harris**, Sales Development Manager,
Colleague and Dear Friend

Bigger Than Sales

How Humility and Relationships Build Career Success

Chip Helm

Bigger Than Sales:
How Humility and Relationships Build Career Success

By Chip Helm
© 2018, 2019 Chip Helm

Printed in the United States of America

All rights reserved sole by the author. The author guarantees all contents are original and do not infringe upon the legal rights of any other person or work. No part of this book may be reproduced, stored in a retrieval system, or transmitted in any form or by any means without expressed written permission of the author.

In Association with:
Elite Online Publishing
63 East 11400 South #230
Sandy, UT 84070

Editorial Director: Dr. Larry Keefauver
Cover/Text Design/Layout: Lisa Simpson

ISBN: 978-1099161896

Dedication

I hope by now you have read about my "K.I.S.S. Method" dedication to God, Cyrilla, and my children, in "Everyday Sales Wisdom for Life & Career." Without God and my loving family, I would not have written either of my two books, and that is a given!

You now would not be on this page of this new book, "Bigger Than Sales: How Humility and Relationships Build Career Success," if not for being gracious or kind, or maybe just maybe I was able to serve you, and something I have said has hit home and made an impact on you. Like I have always said, if I have helped one person like you, I win!

I wanted to give a shout out to my parents, Bud and Betty Helm, who both are deceased. I know my Dad is upstairs playing golf, and my mom is still having her wonderful dinner parties; and like her son, never met a stranger!

Thank you to the best parents a son could have. Between the mentoring I received from my Father and the skills to engage people from my Mother, I am the luckiest son on Earth! I love you both dearly and miss you both with all my heart!

Acknowledgments

Obviously, my loving family will always be acknowledged when I do anything in life; especially when being so blessed to write a book about *Humility and Relationships*. Thank you Cyrilla, Matthew, Michaela, Sam, and even Mac, our Great Dane, who along with my other Danes growing up taught me a lot about humility, caring, and love.

Is it okay to admit I have loved my Great Danes more than some people; or is that TMI, or just too much honesty?

But be patient with me because I want to say **thank you** to a few other people for helping me, contributing to, and believing in me to write this book.

First of all, Ramon Avila, Professor of Sales & Marketing at Ball State, who gave me my first opportunity to get up in front of a class of students five years ago; you know how hard it is to engage college students.

Second, Dick Canada and Charlie Ragland, both professors at the Center for Global Sales leadership at Kelly School of Business at Indiana University who gave me an opportunity to share and mentor their students in their sales classes

Third, Dan McQuiston, Professor of Sales and Marketing at Butler University, who called me one day and asked me to share my personal branding story with his class. Hopefully, the personal branding chapter is as impactful to you as it is for me because I lived it, and then wrote about it, and have delivered it to many audiences.

Last but not least, or better yet maybe I saved the best for last, I have the best editor/publicist/publisher duo in the world!

Thank you Dawn Mitchell and Larry Keefauver, for the privilege and honor to have you both on my team to be the best I can be, and to make sure my voice resonated throughout these books. If anyone out there reading these books wants the best of the best if you decide to write a book, Dawn and Larry are #1 in my book, no pun intended. And that is a fact!

Table of Contents

Introduction – Find Your Passion 13

Chapter 1 – Communicate Effectively... 17

Chapter 2 – Lead by Humility 31

Chapter 3 – Master the Art of Networking................................... 43

Chapter 4 – Develop Personal Branding....................................... 53

Chapter 5 – Choose the Right Company 69

Chapter 6 – Cultivate a Healthy Work/Life Balance 83

Final Word – Keep Growing.. 91

Appendix 1 – Resources You Really Need! 93

Appendix 2 – Rules of Engagement... 105

Appendix 3 – "Chipisms" 107

Connect with Chip Helm 118

Introduction

Find Your Passion

"If you don't love what you do,
you won't do it with much conviction or passion"
—**Mia Hamm**

I have been truly fortunate because I fell in love with what I do. Finding my passion, I ran with it. Vision inspires passion which fuels purpose, plans, and productivity.

When you are passionate, you don't let yourself fail even when you are out of gas! Statistics report that most people never have just one passion, I have been so fortunate to have three passions inspired by my faith-based vision—my family, my home in Northern Michigan, and selling for Cook Medical.

If I could bottle up passion, and sell it across this country, I would. Passion is…

infectious,
　　inspiring,
　　　　infusing,
　　　　　　impacting,
　　　　　　　　incendiary,
　　　　　　　　　　energizing,

> *mobilizing,*
> *compelling,*
> *empowering,*
> *and **winning**!*

Ultimately, passion is a primary driving force behind success and happiness allowing us to live better lives and better the lives of others. Passion will even move you beyond success to significance.

How do you find your passion?

☐ Following your dream drives passion.

☐ Loving what you do will drive you to become passionate.

☐ Positive attitude will open doors and lead to finding your passion.

☐ Your hobby can be a strong passion for you.

☐ Write down a list of goals. One of those goals could become a passion.

☐ Mentors can guide you down the passion pathway.

☐ Your gut will be a leader in driving you towards your passion.

☐ Sometimes others try to stop you because they think they know what's best for you. Listen to your inner self; not to others. ***Pursue your true God-given passion.***

As you can read in my first book, "Everyday Sales Wisdom for Your Life & Career," you discover that my journey has checked most of the boxes above. Mentors guided me, I have been goal-oriented my entire life, and I fell in love with what I do.

Once you have identified your true passion, you need to begin to work toward becoming the best you can be at what you do. This book is designed to give you the tools to do just that.

> **"Nothing is as important as passion.**
> **No matter what you want to do with your life,**
> **be passionate."**
>
> —Jon Bon Jovi

Chapter 1

Communicate Effectively

> *Do More…*
> *Do more than exist—live.*
> **Do more than hear—listen.**
> *Do more than agree—cooperate.*
> **Do more than talk—communicate…**
> *Do more than work—excel…*
> *Do more than share—give…*
> **Do more than help—serve.**
> *Do more than coexist—reconcile…*
> *Do more than advise—help…*
> *Do more than encourage—inspire.*
> *Do more than add—multiply.*
> *Do more than change—improve.*
> *Do more than reach—stretch."*
> —**John Mason,** "You Can Do It--
> Even if Others Say You Can't"[1]

Re-read and then memorize John Mason's imperative, particularly…*Do more than hear—listen…do more than talk…communicate!*

Communication is so critical for all your relationships—family, friends, and career with both your colleagues and your customers or clients. It is the biggest asset and also the biggest pitfall we have, but many people are lacking in communication skills.

These are Chip Helm's three C's of Communication:

- **Consistent Communication**
- **Constant Communication**
- **Correct Communication**

Consistent Communication: Consistant communication is continual…ongoing…seamless…unbroken. Long periods of silence are often perceived by others (remember perception is reality) as inactivity, unproductiveness, and "you are too busy for them." To be honest with you, most bosses will think you are hiding from them or don't want to speak to them the longer you go without speaking. It really can make the next time you either run into each other or talk to each other uncomfortable to say the least.

Treat folks the same no matter what day of the week they approach you about anything. It should not matter if your employee walks in Tuesday morning or Thursday morning, you should respond the same way regardless of the question or request. What you don't want to hear around the water cooler is your subordinates whispering; "Don't walk into their office right now, not a good time, try them tomorrow." It just should not matter the day or time of day when an employee has a question, concern or request. Handle it consistently, and with humility. In fact, treat them like you want to be treated.

Be self-aware about how you treat and communicate with your colleagues, your employees, your boss, and your customers. The key is to constantly "check in" with them and ask them if you are consistent in your communication with them. Learn by observation. Be honest and transparent with them.

Obviously, it is important for it to be a three-way communication between you, your colleagues, and your boss working together to be more consistent in the communication within the company.

When it comes to consistent communication with your customers, be dependable and reliable. Follow the "Chipisms," **"Do what you say you will do when you say you will do it" and "Honesty is always the best policy."** Checking in with them regularly shows them your willingness to be available to help them solve problems. Answer their calls and contacts immediately if possible, but make it your policy to respond within twenty-four hours.

Constant Communication: Are you having constant communication with your boss and colleagues? Constant communication in the corporate world can be a challenge because we are all busy, and we get caught up in what is going on from day to day. We are in our own world, trying to solve our world problems, and we forget that we have people around us that can help us, need us, and give us some good advice.

The key is to start having regular meetings with your colleagues, but don't overdo it. Have an agenda so you don't have a meeting just to have a meeting to hear yourself talk. If you don't start having meetings or as I call them "get togethers," you won't ever get to good, sound, constant communication. You don't have to have formal meetings; you can meet for breakfast or lunch, or you can meet after work for a drink. The more you can try to get together, the stronger the relationship becomes, and you end up really enjoying working with each other. Getting together for an occasional social outing strengthens the bond, increases loyalty, and will even increase productivity at work. Remember, it is always about people.

When you have your meetings or get togethers, always make sure you listen to each other and respect what each of you is saying. If you do that, then everyone will enjoy the constant communication.

Finally, maybe the most important element to good constant communication is honesty and transparency with every communication you have with each other. You must always feel safe that each of you can "speak your piece" and still feel respected and heard.

When it comes to constant communication with your customers, it is important to keep your name "in front of them." You can do this by making periodic phone calls and using some of today's technology to remind them you are out there and willing to help with their problems. Of course, scheduling regular face-to-face meetings with them is essential to keeping the lines of communication open with them. Be available to them through e-mails and texts as well and follow the guidelines below of correct communication.

Correct Communication: This can be very complicated, but it's important and necessary to understand because it rules our world on an everyday basis whether it is an e-mail, text, phone call, face-to-face, or through social media. Correct communication is caring.

As far as I am concerned, face-to-face will always be "the best of the best" form of communication. That is how you build a strong relationship! I am still going to buy from whom I like. I am still going to want to know who you are, and you are not going to have that by texting and e-mailing the person. You can't really get to know a person unless you are sitting across from them, and you can see their eyes, watch their body language, and listen to how well they speak. The other person is "interviewing" you, too. They want to figure you out as much as you want to figure them out.

Though face-to-face is the ideal form of communication, in this world today with costs and expenses to be considered, you may have to consider using other modes of communication. Your initial meeting with a customer should be face-to-face if at all possible. I would go one step further and suggest if you can meet them another couple of times face-to-face as you begin your relationship and develop that partnership, that would be ideal!

We need to move on to the good, bad, and ugly of e-mails and text messages. Here are some "Don'ts" in writing e-mails:

#1- Never mention negative feelings or thoughts, and never provide negative input even though you feel it is constructive criticism. Keep your emotions out of your e-mails.

#2- Do not tell your life story. Keep e-mails succinct and to the point.

#3- Do not react immediately to a nasty e-mail. Take a deep breath and wait 24 hours before you send it.

Correct communication is caring. You project with the tone of your words that you are truthful, empathetic, transparent, and respectful. You are inviting a response from that person not trying to shut him/her down. If it has taken a lot of back and forth to try to resolve an issue through an e-mail, pick up the phone. You can usually solve a problem in a minute or two and avoid letting the discussion get way out of hand. Once you push the send button for the e-mail, there is no turning back, and it will always be out there! With all the regulations and compliance issues within today's corporate world, you need to be very careful what you put in writing. They can even be used against you in a court of law.

However, an e-mail is perfect and ideal for a good follow up in between the first time you meet someone face-to-face and the next time you meet. By following up, I mean to make sure you are both on the same page with what you discussed face-to-face or through a phone call. Did you make any promises? Restate them so there is no miscommunication about what and when you will fulfill those promises. What were your action items? Clarify things you need to do and things they need to do. An e-mail is also a perfect follow up to both a phone call and face-to-face meeting to say "Thank you" for their time and their business.

Another good use of an e-mails is when you are unable to see someone for a while. It keeps you in front of the customer. They get a friendly reminder that you are still around. Always keep in touch, no matter what form of communication you use, just do it.

E-mails are fantastic to use to introduce yourself to a new customer or colleague. I believe a great way to begin a relationship is to write an introductory e-mail, but keep it concise and to the point. There may be situations where the only way to get an appointment is by writing an e-mail. Used properly, e-mails allow us to conduct business with our customers much more efficiently.

Here are some tips for writing an introductory e-mail to get a meeting with a customer:

- Take a writing class and concentrate on writing essays, resumes, and cover letters.

- Be concise, to the point, and be very caring, thoughtful, and kind. "Kill with kindness."

- Don't leave the e-mail open-ended. You want a yes or no response.

- Pick one product to ask for a meeting to discuss.

- Do research on the customer so you can include a personal comment.

- Ask for advice, input, and use words like, "I know you are busy, but could you be so kind as to spare a few minutes…"

- Use referrals or name drop if you can.

- Make the person feel like a King or Queen. Read it back to yourself, the e-mail should jump at you that you made them feel special.

- Don't send an e-mail with even a few typos or grammatical mistakes. Re-read it before you push send. Sometimes one small error can change the whole meaning of your e-mail. A well-written, thoughtful e-mail that thinks of the customer first may very well secure you an appointment!

People sometimes write e-mails with sentence fragments, are wordy, or too business like. You should put some healthy positive emotion into every e-mail written to a customer. Here is the ultimate key with customer e-mails: "Business is always personal" so craft an e-mail with "a personal touch."

Is texting a correct communication today? Most young adults would say yes! Texting is usually short and gets to the point. Some people do not respond as fast with e-mails as they do with a text message, so depending on the information you want or how fast you want an answer to a question, a text over an e-mail may be a better form of communication.

The downside with texting is it can be misinterpreted. You cannot judge their reaction like you can with a face-to-face communication.

I am not a fan of the acronyms like "lol" because many of them can be interpreted in different types of ways. You must read your audience in sales, preferably through an initial face-to-face contact, then you will know if it is appropriate to use text messaging versus e-mails for follow ups and setting future appointments. Find that out up front so your communication will be correct for your audience.

My least desirable form of communication is "Social Media" because it has been overused for all the wrong reasons. I see people posting very personal and private pictures when they are trying to get a job. It's true some companies have hired people because of social media, but more importantly they have fired people because of it. Be aware, companies do use social media sites to research a candidate that they are looking to hire. Be sure they are not going to find out something about you that would be detrimental to your being considered as a future employee.

"6 Ground Rules" of Direct Report/ Employee Relationships

These are important communication "Ground Rules" when meeting with the person who is your Direct Report (DR):

1) **Types of Communication/ How responsive is your communication/How often**

    a) Does your Direct Report like e-mail, text or phone?

    b) How frequently does your DR respond to texts, e-mails, phone?

    c) How often does your DR want to hear from you; weekly, bi-weekly, or ____?

Communicate Effectively

    d) Does your DR enjoy communication – laugh, have fun, and want to talk to each other?

2) **Autonomy**

    a) Gives you room (space) to manage your own region or territory.

    b) Allows you to make the decisions, and allows you to decide how to manage your region, territory, etc.

    c) Gives you freedom to express yourself and take ownership.

3) **Type of management style**

    a) Micro-Manager

    b) Hands-off Manager

    c) Delegator, mentor type

4) **Expectations**

    a) How can I help you (DR) be successful?

    b) This is what I need from you to be successful.

5) **Professional Development**

    a) Will they help you grow; get you where you want to get?

    b) Will DR be supportive of outside interests (taking PD courses, "Giving back to Community" projects)?

6) **Honesty and transparency**

    a) Can you have that open and honest conversation?

    b) No one takes it personal, and you make up every time.

c) Honest and transparency are a 2-way street.

This "Ground Rules" concept was graciously given to me by Caroline Dowd-Higgins, a published author and leadership Coach at Indiana University.

For many, if not all of us at some point in our careers, we usually have bosses, whom I call "Direct Reports." **It is critical to set the "ground rules" at the beginning of the DR/employee relationship.**

I really believe most people do not ever consider discussing "Ground Rules" with their DR because it is their boss, and they are just supposed to do what they are told.

"Ground Rules" concept is a ground-breaking tool to help anyone have a better working relationship with their boss/DR.

In my thirty-two years, it is all about who you report to! A DR can make you or break you. So, sit down at beginning of your relationship; it will make a difference. Look at it this way; "No harm, no foul. If you don't like what your Direct Report says, at least you know exactly how to work with them—good or bad!

My Top 3 No-No's with Social Media

#1- Do not post private and personal pictures on any social media site.

#2- Do not post religious and political views on social media sites.

#3- Do not post private and personal comments specific to health issues.

I am concerned for people who are looking for a job, and more importantly want to keep their job! Be careful with any social media sites because once you push the send button, it is always out there in space. You can't take back what you said, and if you are not careful, you can hurt yourself and possibly a lot of other people as well.

It would not be fair to end this chapter without giving you all the Do's for Social Media:

#1- Great sites to catch up with old friends, meet new friends, and keep up with what is going on with the kids.

#2- Linkedin is my favorite site. It is a great site for professionals.

#3- Social Media is an excellent venue to market your company, your products, and yourself. I buy many things through Social Media.

#4- Social Media is great for small businesses to get free marketing.

Communication Networking

Networking is an important part of sales. Good communication is essential as you develop your networking skills. Start by buying a notebook to keep notes on all the connections you make. Keep 2-3 personal notes about each person you meet and connect with during the day. Google to see if you can put a picture to a name. Be diligent to record daily your new contacts. Separate them into three categories: Colleagues, Customers, and Family/ Friends. Review your notebook weekly to learn and remember their names.

1. Start networking by putting your hand out, have good eye contact, and just introduce yourself. This is usually very uncomfortable for most people. Go out of your way to meet

five new people daily. Don't walk away without an e-mail address or cell phone number.

2. Face-to-face networking, e-mails, text messages, and phone follow ups. Follow up will be key as you build your network of over fifty people. Prioritize whom you need to follow up with in person every one to two months.

3. Make this a game to see how many new people in your three categories you can meet, get reacquainted with, or just build a stronger relationship.

4. Start with your colleagues at work or your family and friends who already like you.

Know your audience. I was at a medical meeting and ran into a good friend of mine, Glen Deyo. We began discussing communication styles. The reason this became a topic for discussion was because I had just e-mailed a surgeon friend of mine, more than a couple of times trying to see him at this meeting. I was getting kind of frustrated because I had known this surgeon for around thirty years and wondered why he had not responded to my e-mails.

I told my friend what had happened after I had been there for about a day or so. I saw this surgeon from a distance and proceeded to go over and track him down, my networking skill at its best. We started talking, and since I have known him for many years, I just blurted out, "Why didn't you ever get back to me? I e-mailed you two or three times trying to connect with you while we at this meeting."

He shook his head and answered, "I get 10,000 e-mails daily and do not have time to respond. Text me because I will answer those more often."

He gave me his cell number and I texted him in the morning to set up a time to meet. I was skeptical that he would really reply to my text, but he texted me back and we were able to get together.

I told my friend Glen, I always thought or assumed that only millennials texted; not old people like me who are over fifty. Glen said it is in fact very common for professional people over fifty who are very busy and just don't have time to reply to all their e-mails to rely on texting for better communication. Since texting comes up on the front of their phones, they see it, and you have a much better chance to hear from them.

Take home message: Ask people how they want to communicate! Don't assume you know. If you find out they are texters, make sure you get their cell number before you walk away.

Take this message to the bank:
Ask people how they want to communicate!
Don't assume you know!

It always pays to know how others want to communicate and to do it their way instead of insisting on your way.

DEVELOPING COMMUNICATION SKILLS

Since communication is such an important part of our personal and professional lives, take a moment and read through these suggestions for developing or improving yours.

One good way to develop communication skills is to take a course. I took the Dale Carnegie course years ago. The Dale Carnegie course teaches you to get up in front of people and speak and to learn how to speak impromptu.

IMPROVE YOUR WRITING/ GRAMMAR SKILLS

- *Take a writing class and concentrate on writing essays, resumes, and cover letters.*

- *There are also writing classes you can take specifically in conjunction with sales.*

- *Spend time writing e-mails and letters to improve those skills.*

- *Use spell-check or a tool like Grammarly.*

Chapter 2

Lead by Humility

"Humility is the most important quality for somebody who wants to be president. I think it's really important to know what you don't know and listen to people who know what you don't know."
—**George W. Bush** (CNBC interview July 14, 2017)

It's important that you realize you are leading people every day regardless if you have people who report directly to you or are influencing colleagues, family, and friends through being a good servant and mentor.

I believe sales is the foundation necessary to hold any other future positions in your company. If you are fortunate enough to have begun your career in sales, you will have learned relationship skills, how to navigate the competitive landscape, the importance of product knowledge, and that "the customer is always right." The most important skill you have learned, though, is that "it's all about the customer." If you always put the customer first, you will be better prepared than most for leadership positions within your company.

The one major caveat to that, however, is that not all great sales people make good leaders. It is more common than not that your best sales people are not the best at leading people. However, if you have sales as a foundation, you will be a better leader because you will understand the importance of building relationships and treating people like you want to be treated.

As you have probably already discovered, this is a book about more than sales. Obviously, you will learn skills that you can use in sales, but you are really learning life lessons that can provide you with greater opportunities to serve others in any of your leadership positions. The bottom line is, if at all possible, spend some time in sales. That foundation will make you a great leader, but an even better person.

Second on my list of how to be a great leader is you always want to have goals. If you don't have goals that you want to achieve and you're not always trying to improve, you may not end up in a leadership role. No matter how hard you try or how driven you are, if you don't have clearly defined goals you will flounder. I am a great example of always being goal driven. When I was out in field sales, I used to tell them I would be a manager in four years. Though it didn't happen in four years, ten years later I fulfilled that goal and became a Sales Manager.

Working as a sales person, having goals, and working at achieving those goals will give you the best chance to succeed at a leadership position.

Another very important part of becoming a great leader is to realize, "It is not what you say, it's how you say things." You can be a tough leader who has to make hard decisions, but you can make those decisions with kindness. You don't have to do it with "an iron fist"! I call what we need to be "leadership with humility." Another way to put it is learn to "use soft skills" to get what you need accomplished. No one uses empathy or sympathy much anymore in dealing with people, but those are worthwhile skills to employ if you want to become effective in leadership. If you live by the credence, "treat people like you want to be treated," you will probably end up in any leadership position you desire.

An ancient proverb observes, "Pride comes before a fall." How true. Pride can kill a sale, a relationship, and even a career. Being self-centered means the relationship is "all about me." Humility projects the perception that this relationship is "all about you." Simply put, "Get over yourself." Or, you might redefine K.I.S.S. as Keep It Simply Selfless.

What a Great Sales Leader Looks Like

A great sales leader is **consistent** day in and day out. A great leader **respects** everyone. People want a leader that is always working on their behalf, wants to try to get them where they want to go, and helps to make them successful. People want their leader to put them in positions that can showcase their strengths and minimize their weaknesses. They want a leader who will help them develop professionally.

A great leader **serves others** by putting others first and is consistently honest and transparent. A great leader also has excellent **soft skills**—empathy, sympathy, appropriate tone, delivers instructions and especially correction with kindness and humbleness. Some call this having the attitude of a servant leader. Again, ancient wisdom reminds us that *the person who would be great must become a servant* and *those who would be first, let them become last.*

Most people do not like to work for a micro-manager. They would prefer a leader act as a mentor that helps them constantly improve and learn to discover their potential.

There is a great book out called, "Ideal Team Players" where they look at a person with the following qualities: Humble, determined, interpersonal skills, hungry, and smart. What they concluded was if you were humble, interpersonal, and hungry, or humble, interpersonal, and determined, you will be successful in life. If you were interpersonal, hungry, and determined, you would not do very well.

Humility has to be one of your primary attributes to be successful!

If a person is not humble, that person isn't someone you would want in your company. We have had interviews where we feel the person has checked off all the boxes except for the humble box and they did not get hired. How did we uncover that the person did not have the "humble card"? We asked many humble type questions and they failed the litmus test. I will include a list of interview questions at end of the book.

BEING HUMBLE IS NOT ROCKET SCIENCE

You treat people like you want to be treated. It is as simple as that, no more, no less. Use the word "We and not I." Desire to serve others, be a good listener, and put people into positions to succeed. People will enjoy working for a leader who devotes energy and time to help them get where they want to go and not worry about themselves.

Leadership by humility involves being aware of how you "say" things whether it is verbally, e-mailing, or texting. You and I can say the same thing, but I can say it differently and it may be better received than how you say it. It is all in the delivery and the tone of your voice. That is where soft skills come to play. Leading by humility involves good communication skills.

A good sales leader does not micromanage. I love that term because it clearly expresses the word picture that someone is "in your business." Micromanagement is a management style whereby a manager closely observes and/or controls the work of his/her subordinates or employees. Micromanagement is generally considered to have a negative connotation, mainly because it shows a lack of freedom in the workplace.

A good sales leader stays out of their staff's business unless it is really needed because they are not doing very well on their own. When they are having trouble, or they ask for help, use soft skills in guiding and leading them rather than "managing" them. Ask questions and discover how you can be a resource and how can you help them through the discovery process. If you don't micromanage, you could be on your way to becoming a great leader. Surround yourself with good people, let them do their thing, and stay out of their way. You will just mess it up if you micromanage.

Leadership doesn't always mean having "Direct Reports." You can still be a good leader and not have people report directly to you. A friend of mine told me, "You can still influence people no matter what you are doing. You don't have to have direct reports to make an impact on your colleagues, family, and friends."

Average leaders play checkers and great leaders play chess. What does this mean? In checkers, all the pieces are uniform and move in the same way; they are somewhat interchangeable. You need to plan and coordinate their movements, certainly, but they all move at the same pace on parallel paths.

In chess, each distinct piece moves in a different way, and you can't play if you don't know how each piece moves. More importantly, you won't win if you don't think carefully about how you move the pieces. Chess is like "leading a team" since there are all different pieces, all different people, going different ways, so you have to have more strategies. You have to understand your people and you have to read your people. That is how you are going to be a more successful leader.

> Chess is a perfect example of what makes a sales person a great leader!

Great leaders look at people's strengths and not their weaknesses. Weaknesses are minimized when people know and build upon their strengths. Many books describe methods to improve your weaknesses, but that is certainly not the best way to move forward in your career. When people are asked by their bosses to take their weaknesses or things they don't do well and try to change them, they will spend too much time working on what they don't do well instead of recognizing and developing their strengths. We were most likely hired because of our strengths, not our weaknesses. As a leader, encourage your people to improve and develop their strengths instead of focusing on their weaknesses. You will have a much happier and more productive team if you do. In fact, if you help them get more training to unleash their strength potential, your team will flourish.

The other thing I want to emphasize is we would not have leadership responsibility if not for our "sales people." We should think about how we can help those we have oversight of directly or indirectly over day in and day out. No company would be around without their soldiers (sales people). You are there to help them succeed and will thereby help your company succeed as well. One effective and humble salesman I know has this motto: *Make money. Influence people.*

Not all great sales people make good leaders, but all sales people can still be great influencers.

There are two ways of leading people. You have direct reports that you guide, coach, and develop with humility. You also influence your colleagues through humility and mentoring. You are leading people every day regardless if you have direct reports or are influencing colleagues through being a good servant leader and mentor.

Remember, when it is all said and done, you are always trying to get better as a person by "treating people like you want to be treated." True leadership is when you are humble and are in service to others. When you do, you are at the greatest leadership level!

John Maxwell writes and speaks volumes about servant leadership. Here's a list of some of his statements. Take a moment. Rate yourself from 0 to 10 on each statement. Be honest and humble. Then ask some colleagues, friends and family to rate you. Compare their perceptions of you to your own. Go to work on growing and getting better in the areas others score you lowest.

— I believe the bottom line in leadership isn't how far we advance ourselves but how far we advance others. That is achieved by serving others and adding value to their lives.

— If you are a leader, then trust me, you are having either a positive or a negative impact on the people you lead. How can you tell? There is one critical question: Are you making things better for the people who follow you?

— Being an "adder" requires me to get out of my comfort zone every day and think about adding value to others. But that's what it takes to be a leader whom others want to follow.

— The best place for a leader isn't always the top position. It isn't the most prominent or powerful place. It's the place where he or she can serve the best and add the most value to other people.

— Great leadership means great service.

— When you add value to people, you lift them up, help them advance, make them a part of something bigger than themselves, and assist them in becoming who they were made to be.

— Effective leaders go beyond not harming others, and they intentionally help others. To do that, they must value people and demonstrate that they care in such a way that their followers know it.

— Leaders who add value by serving believe in their people before their people believe in them and serve others before they are served.

— Inexperienced leaders are quick to lead before knowing anything about the people they intend to lead. But mature leaders listen, learn, and then lead. They listen to their people's stories. They find out about their hopes and dreams. They become acquainted with their aspirations. And they pay attention to their emotions. From those things, they learn about their people. They discover what is valuable to them. And then they lead based upon what they've learned.

— I believe that God desires us not only to treat people with respect, but also to actively reach out to them and serve them.

— *Total*

(Your total is _____. By the way, there are ten statements which means the highest score is 100. Is your total a passing score of 70 or above? How others score you can be a good reality check for you.)

Humility and Leadership

Are you able to be empathetic and sympathetic but still can make good sound decisions? A definition of leadership by humility is treating people like you want to be treated, using those soft skills, and being empathetic and sympathetic all rolled up into one. You can treat people with kindness and still influence them or lead them to success.

Sales is birthed from humility. If you believe the customer is always right, you will put them first. When you walk in to see them, it will be with humbleness and not arrogance. The humbler and kinder you are with your customers the better your relationship with them and the more sales you will achieve. You will see results.

However, if you are not humble, you don't hear what the people are saying to you, and you can't communicate with them because you come in with a preconceived notion that self-perpetuates itself. You never break through because your arrogance leads you to believe you know it all before you even get there.

Figuring out what the customer really needs so you can serve them is part of humility. You must learn to put aside any personality conflicts and preconceived ideas and treat them like they are a king or queen.

So, the essentials of sales and really in any career are humility, kindness, and service to others. If you want to succeed and move up the ranks in your career, you need to fine tune these skills. I don't believe you will ever be a great leader without humility. I don't believe you will be a great sales person without humility either. The Art of Humility drives great people—leaders, sales people, and in basically any profession!

Leadership by humility also helps us remember a leader doesn't lead alone. Leadership is about influencing others. Just like everyone is in sales, everyone has a sphere of influence whether they realize it or not. We are leaders in our family, our community, and in our business because of the influence we have over those who are observing us. Leadership is a mantle you carry as you journey through your life and career. People will follow leaders who seek to be of service to others.

We don't have enough leaders who "lead by humility." That is why I seek to teach people the importance of humility and how it can impact all those within our sphere of influence. We need to understand that humility is the only way to be a leader and to be a better person.

Everyone needs to take responsibility for the higher calling. I believe God wants us to treat people like we want to be treated. That means treat people with respect, dignity, and become a servant leader. Leadership by Humility needs to become part of everyone's leadership book, training, and part of their DNA.

> A great leader always puts
> the other person first!

As I was thinking about how important it really is to stay humble and kind through the good as well as the bad times in our lives, I heard a Tim McGraw song titled, "Humble and Kind" that really put into words my thoughts. I invite you to check out the words and take his advice to always stay humble and kind.

DEVELOP LEADERSHIP BY HUMILITY

Here are five actions you can take to develop your leadership skills if you aspire to grow to the next level and lead by humility.

1. Get sales experience as your foundation. Start your career in some sort of sales position or seek to cross-train in that area.

2. Hone your soft skills. Take the Dale Carnegie course to understand people. Work on being empathic, sympathetic, and humble.

3. Be a mentor/leader.

4. Know what you stand for.

5. Be humble and kind.

Chapter 3

Master the Art of Networking

"The mark of a good conversationalist is not that you can talk a lot. The mark is that you can get others to talk a lot. Thus, good schmoozers are good listeners, not good talkers."
—Guy Kawasaki

Networking is a lifetime project, a lifetime commitment, and a lifetime journey. You never stop networking throughout your life. It is one of the greatest things you can do. I am still networking to help my son and daughter get into medical school and veterinarian school, respectively. I am always networking. What that means is, if I know someone who knows someone, who knows someone, I will ask them to help get that person a foot in the door and I will always do it to help people. It is what networking is all about.

Today everyone has the same GPA, the same scores, and technical ability, so having someone network in your behalf may make the difference in receiving that sales position or get you into graduate school like my son or daughter. It is definitely who you know.

I had a good friend in college that didn't get into dental school the first time around and realized maybe he should ask for help. His father was a dentist on one of the Indiana Dental boards and helped get his son in. The moral of this story is: *never feel bad that you might not get that job just on your merits; you may need to ask for help to get your foot in the door.*

I look at networking as building your customer base from territory to country to the globe!

You never know who you will meet around the globe that can help you, your friend, or your family. Never stop networking and building the customer base. Developing my network of friends like Bill Armstrong, head of IU foundation, allowed me to get a foot in the door and get my first and only job with Cook Medical.

Networking Tips

Here are some tricks and tips on how you develop networking skills and what you do with them.

Let's start first with my story back in the '80s when I was a sales rep and covered the entire state of Florida. How did I develop a great network of folks across the country?

Tip #1: I would attend meetings and network around the "water cooler," coffee area, or the area where breakfast was being served. Another couple of great places to network were in the hotel lobby where the customers were staying or attending the welcome reception the night before the meeting. At all of these networking events, I would "work the room." I would go from person to person and introduce myself. I would put my hand out, look them directly in the eyes, and introduce myself. I would make a couple of comments with the intent of getting their pagers and e-mail address. Of course today it is a cell phone. I say something that connected them to me and so they would not forget me. I would get around to everyone in the room.

When I got back to my hotel room, I would try put a face to a name. I would write down their name, a couple of notes to remember them, and keep a journal on every single person I met.

When you network, have a firm hand shake that is not gender specific. Direct eye contact is important for excellent face recognition. What is impressive is when you see one of your network "friends" a year or two later and you not only remember the conversation you had earlier, you also have a face recognition. This is because you had good, direct eye contact the last time you met. When you have good face recognition, it makes it much easier when you are in a crowd and you see them off in the distance, especially when you are too far away to see their badge. To be honest, as you get older, you might want to recognize them by face over the small print on a badge that you can't see very well.

It is amazing that most people in general are afraid of putting their hand out and introducing themselves to a stranger. You must learn the technique of putting "your hand out" and "saying hello." It is uncomfortable to put your hand out and say hello to a stranger, but it is an essential skill in the art of networking. Like everything in life, it is all about "preparation, preparation, preparation." So, before I go to an event, I research and know my audience. I know who will be there at the event. I have a target list. I have gone through each person on the list and know what I need to talk to them about. I prepare questions like, "Can I catch you in the office tomorrow? Can

I call your secretary?" Have a few questions prepared to get another meeting with them.

Part of my research is to try and get a face to put to each name. Then I have a "face recognition before" I go there. I know what they look like. I don't have to look at their badges or I don't have to look them up. I do a lot of my homework before I go to make sure I network as successfully as I can.

You invite me over to a party from 7:00-9:00 p.m. When I arrive, I find you have invited twenty-five other people. My goal is to meet every person, if just for a brief but important moment, before 9:00 p.m. When I get home from the party, I get my notebook out, and write down everything I learned from each of my brief meetings. It is critical to keep a notebook for each person. You never know who might become a helpful contact in the future. There are many more facets to networking than selling.

I went to a meeting recently and attended the reception that evening. I should have had a "Fit bit" as I did not stop walking, talking, and introducing myself over the next three hours. I went from one end of the room to the other end and it was a large room. I would stop to talk for a few minutes and then I would go on to the next person and then to the next person. When I ran into a "face recognition" (my term for remembering what they look like), I would stop and spend some quality time with them. That evening or the next morning, I Googled everyone else to get a picture of them. When the meeting was over, I had met and started a file on everyone I possibly could.

Those are the kinds of things you need to do when you go into these events, receptions, and gathering areas. That is how I built my customer base from territory to the country to the globe. I "network the room" the same way every single time. I set up a real direct path and repeat it again and again. It is probably one of my greatest skills. I intentionally and aggressively network a room to get to know people through personal face-to-face contact.

Networking is not a passive sport!

If we think back to our growing up years, we see that networking starts at an early age and never ends. It has been ongoing for me over thirty years. Networking is a process that involves your work ethic, your persistence, and your dedication to go out and meet people. It is simple. "Networking is not rocket science." It is as simple as putting your hand out, looking people in the eyes, and saying hello. It is having a brief conversation with an end goal of meeting people and building your "Globe."

NETWORKING AN EVENT

Preparations before a networking event:

- ➢ Research your audience. Know your audience and know your environment (the event).
- ➢ Put together a hit list; Use Google to help you match a face to a name.

Networking skills to execute always at events:

- ➢ Have a firm handshake.
- ➢ Make direct eye contact.
- ➢ Have a few comments to set up the next time you meet.

- ➢ Hand out business cards and always ask for their business cards.
- ➢ Be "the Great White Shark"— always moving, and meeting people.
- ➢ "Work the room" — never stop moving, have Business cards. Don't stop until you have met as many people as possible.

Great networkers are like the Great White Shark. Sharks never stop moving and great networkers never stop working the room!

While I was at a medical meeting, there was a large decorum area where they had maybe 2,000 physicians. From 6:30 to 9:00 p.m., I never stopped moving. I went from one corner to the next. If I recognized someone or they recognized me, I would stop and have a brief conversation. Then I would move on and basically walked in a circle or in a figure eight so I could cover the whole room. I would continually network the room. I had many brief succinct conversations and made notes in my mind who I talked to and who I hadn't connect with yet. I asked for business cards and gave out my business cards as well.

Depending on the type of event you are attending, go through the program to see the list of speakers, the agenda, the topics, and obtain the attendees list if possible. They could be future customers or people who can help you further down the road in your career. I would wait in the hallway outside the room or even go up to the podium after the speaker spoke at the end of the session to introduce myself. That is how I would put a face to a name. When I saw them speak again or just ran into them at another event, I would go up to them and say hello. It is that simple. A friend of mine once told me, "You have to get uncomfortable to ever get comfortable."

There is nothing better than running into that speaker again at another event and introduce yourself mentioning a previous conversation you had with them. Their eyes will sparkle because you remembered what they told you. Remember, people love to talk about themselves, so encourage them and then keep good records of what you learn. Be a good listener and you will have them where you need them to be, and your relationship is off and running.

Don't forget to reach out by sending a thank you e-mail or a follow-up phone call. It is extremely important to do this within twenty-four to forty-eight hours. I respond to them the very next day whenever possible!

"If You Don't Schmooze, You Lose"

You want to be genuine about your intent to meet people, but you must get out there and schmooze the crowd! Obviously, if you are not genuine and sincere with your actions, people will see right through you. However, you need to be somewhat of a "schmoozer" who gets out there, talks to everyone with a smile, and genuinely wants to get to know people. It is a fine line, but you must get uncomfortable to get comfortable.

A smile is a powerful tool that people do not use enough to their advantage, especially when networking. When people walk up to you with a smile or they walk into a room with a smile, it usually changes the entire dynamics of a conversation.

"If you want to make a good first impression, smile at people. What does it cost to smile? Nothing. What does it cost not to smile? Everything, if not smiling prevents you from enchanting people." —Guy Kawasaki

It would not be right if I did not share about a young lady that works at our company. I will see her every now and then in the hallway and she always has a smile on her face. I mean always! She walks by and generally says, "It is another beautiful day," with her words and her smile. I can't help smiling when I see her and to be honest with you, my day is more fulfilling when I run into her. I can see that smile in my mind and it makes me smile! Smiling is such a powerful tool!

"Good schmoozers give favors. Good schmoozers also return favors. However, great schmoozers ask for the return of favors. You may find this puzzling: Isn't it better to keep someone indebted to you? The answer is no, and this is because keeping someone indebted to you puts undue pressure on your relationship. Any decent person feels guilty and indebted. By asking for, and receiving, a return favor, you clear the decks, relieve the pressure, and set up for a whole new round of give and take. After a few rounds of give and take, you're best friends, and you have mastered the art of schmoozing." —Guy Kawasaki

How I Manage My Database of New Connections/Contacts

- I ask for business cards, and e-mail and cell contact information.
- I hand out as many cards as I collect. Make sure to bring more than enough cards.
- I ask customers to share their contact via V-card through their phone. I open it, save it, and it goes directly to outlook.

- I either use a business card scanner app to scan my cards into contacts in outlook or manually type in the contact information.

- Follow up within twenty-four hours to each new contact via e-mail and/or text.

- I go through my inbox every three weeks to continue communication with new contacts.

- Set up meetings with new contacts within two weeks while it is still fresh in their mind from meeting you.

- Keep all collected business cards for back up.

- Google to get a picture of new contact and add to their information in your ledger.

In his book, *Mr. Schmooze,* Richard Abraham writes that selling is all about relationships and that the consummate salesperson has mastered the secret of *giving, i.e. "…selling is giving. The greatest salespeople actually give for a living."* What are you giving? You're giving your time to listen, communicate, and share what you know and your wisdom with others. I invite you to network with others, build positive relationships, and be willing to give of your time, wisdom, and knowledge to serve others.

The Art of Networking

Here are five things you can do right now to build/refresh/or nurture your network.

1. Work on using a firm hand shake, direct eye contact, and put your other hand on the person's shoulder as you shake their hand (men to men and women to women).

2. Meet five new people daily.

3. Learn "face recognition." Put a face with a name (develop recognition skill).

4. Start keeping a ledger/notebook to make notes on every meeting.

5. Know your audience by researching the audience before going to an event.

Chapter 4

Develop Personal Branding

*"It takes a lifetime to build a good reputation,
but you can lose it in a minute."*
—Will Rogers[10]

Attending a professional development course on personal branding, I was really struck by how valuable personal branding is to employees. Yet, it does not appear that many employees are getting training on what peers and leadership think their personal branding is, how to develop it, and how to change what is possibly holding them back in the business world.

Personal branding was popularized in an article by Tom Peters in *Fast Company Magazine* ("A Brand Called You") over ten years ago. He starts out the article by writing, "Regardless of age, regardless of position, regardless of the business we happen to be in, all of us need to understand the importance of branding. We are CEOs of our own companies: Me, Inc. To be in business today, our most important job is to be head marketer for the brand called You."

Personal branding is the practice of people marketing themselves and their careers as "brands." While previous self-help management techniques were about self-*improvement*, the personal-branding concept suggests instead that success comes from self-*packaging*.

Personal Brand = Your Reputation

My thirty-two-year sales career has gone through a lot of ups and downs with my personal branding. I have always had a consistent, honest, passionate, sincere, and very responsive personal branding. What happens, though, it takes people like me many years to build a positive personal branding, but only an hour to lose it.

I wish I'd gone through a personal branding course thirty-two years ago. Maybe I would have ended up in the same place, but at least I would have had more self-awareness and maybe made less mistakes. In the corporate world, it is all about what others perceive; especially folks in leadership positions. It really does not matter what you think your brand is or should be. It only takes one unfavorable situation to take your brand down and turn your world upside down. Unfortunately, everything good you have done is forgotten and what you did wrong or others perceived you did wrong is all people remember.

I went through some situations early in my career where I was not very self-aware of my surroundings and my audience. I said things that were taken out of context. These situations occurred at business meetings and sales events. It is very important to understand your audience to the point of staying away from any personal and confrontational topics. Also, don't disclose too much; not everyone is going to understand you, or they may think you are providing TMI (too much information). A good friend said it best about me; I am an acquired taste. Not everyone is going to like me right off the bat, but as you get to know me, you'll love me because I care, have a big heart, and as honest as the day is long.

Most of my "situations" occurred when I was blind-sided because I had no idea that what I said was offensive or taken the wrong way or perceived as not what I meant. I am too honest, love to kid people, and will walk into a group conversation and join it like they are my close personal friends. Don't do that! Always be aware of your surroundings. Speak less and listen more. My honesty, energy, and love for people got the best of me more than once. I have lost a lot of sleep over these mistakes because I didn't intentionally want to make them. What happens, though, is it puts you back a ton in people's minds because they won't remember all the great things about you; they will just remember what you did wrong.

Let me say right up front, I take complete ownership of my actions and have never blamed anyone else or made excuses. I have made plenty of mistakes, but I have never said or done anything to people with a malicious intent or not the right heart. However, here is what my experience and know how tells me. There are people who don't want you to get where you want to go because they are either intimidated, jealous or not good leaders/mentors. Sometimes the truth hurts, but it is the real world and I don't believe it is going to change anytime soon.

No one wishes more than I do that I had not lacked so much self-awareness that I could make these types of mistakes. Learn from mine and don't make these same mistakes.

This all came to a head one day, when a student in my class asked, "Mr. Helm, when did you develop your personal brand?"

Dumbfounded, I paused and then admitted, "I never developed my brand until many years into my job."

Looking back, I told him I wish I'd developed my brand right out of the gate as I started my career. I proceeded to tell the class that the only reason I woke up and began to "worry" and want to understand my brand is when I got knocked off the corporate ladder one day and hit the ground very hard. I thought I was moving up the corporate ladder, but in a flash, I lost whatever brand I had, even though I didn't know what it was at the time.

What knocked me off my "pedestal" or what I now refer to as a very tall ladder, was my lack of self-awareness. I did not know my audience! I was at a National Sales Meeting and at the bar with many people having a good time. I was not aware who was sitting around me or within hearing distance. Apparently, I said something that must have offended someone, and boy, did I did hear about it later! I am still not sure I really said anything wrong, but it does not matter. Others who could impact my career thought I said something wrong, that was all that mattered. In retrospect, I should have sized up my audience, kept my mouth shut, listened, and smiled rather than commenting on everything else that was said.

These turned into great learning experiences because in the real world, these situations happen all the time. I learned to understand them, learn from them, and be better for it. To be honest, it could have been worse for me. I have learned from these experiences and now share with others that we must be careful with our tongues as there are always people listening and watching us.

A good side note here is the less you drink in the business meetings the better. When we drink, we all get looser with our language, share TMI (too much information), and we don't think about others around us. You may have had only one drink the entire evening, but that does not matter because it is people's perception of your condition that matters. If you get into a lively discussion and share

TMI, people might think you've had more than one drink. A great friend of mine taught me a golden rule: If you drink, just don't do it at business events.

Your Personal Brand

As I inferred in the story above, your reputation or your personal brand is directly influenced by what people perceive or their impression of you. Your brand is defined by your actions and your words. Everything you say and do influences what people think of you. People make mental notes about you every time they interact with you. That means every interaction builds your brand. Your brand is also reflected in your promise, your pledge, and what you stand for.

Positive brands would be for people to perceive you as consistent, sincere, genuine, a good leader, listener, strategic, not a micromanager, and accessible.

Negative brands are micromanager, talks too much, doesn't listen, arrogant, not accessible, not a mentor, and rogue.

Personal Branding Leads to Professional Opportunities

The undeniable truth is your next raise and job promotion will hinge on what your boss thinks of you. You need to check in quarterly to see how you are doing. Industry recognition is a feather in your cap because when your colleagues from other companies think you are good at what you do; you are! They watch you at meetings interact with their customers and they hear from customers how good you are.

Customer recognition is the cream of the cream as far as measuring your performance and success in your career. When customers recognize you as the best of the best, that is what it is all about. If you were not concerned about raises and job promotions, customer recognition would be #1 in importance to measuring your success. Usually customer recognition or satisfaction equates to success.

Finding a mentor will help you develop a good brand for yourself. They can be truthful with you and can assess what your brand is and what your brand may not be. Here are five questions you should ask your mentor to help identify you brand.

#1 - What do you think my brand is?

#2 - What can I do to fix or improve my brand?

#3 - Give me some advice on what to watch out for in the corporate world?

#4 - What are the top five attributes of the ideal brand?

#5 - How do I align my brand with my Direct Report?

All aspects of your personal brand are important!

Before I get into the importance of self-awareness and self-perception, the little things that people don't think about like body language and the way you dress contribute to better self-awareness. Your body language is so important when you are speaking to people, when you are walking around your company or our seeing customers. Good eye contact, a firm handshake, and a smile on your face go a long way toward creating a positive branding. A friend of mine mentioned he was told when he crossed his arms, people felt he cared and he was intently listening to what they were saying. I caught myself crossing my arms one day while I was standing up and listening to a colleague talk to me. Try it sometime and see what people say to your "branding."

Secondly, dress appropriately. It makes a big difference as to how people perceive you; especially in interviews, sales meetings, and meeting with customers. I don't believe you can over-dress. It is the inappropriate or underdressed for the occasion that can set you back. Remember, you want your brand aligned with your boss' work ethics. Body language and how you are dressed are small things, but to me you have no chance to improve or create your brand if you are not self-aware enough to work on your dress and body language. You can easily correct those subtle parts of your brand.

> "That cross-trainer you're wearing — one look at the distinctive swoosh on the side tells everyone who's got you branded. That coffee travel mug you're carrying — ah, you're a Starbucks woman! Your T-shirt with the distinctive Champion "C" on the sleeve, the blue jeans with the prominent Levi's rivets, the watch with the hey-this-certifies-I-made-it icon on the face, your fountain pen with the maker's symbol crafted into the end …You're branded, branded, branded, branded." — Tom Peters

Self-awareness!

Self-awareness is the key cornerstone to emotional intelligence according to Daniel Goleman. The ability to monitor our emotions and thoughts from moment to moment is key to understanding ourselves better, being at peace with who we are, and proactively managing our thoughts, emotions, and behaviors. In addition, self-aware people tend to act consciously rather than react passively, to be in good psychological health, and to have a positive outlook on life. They also have greater depth of life experience and are more likely to be more compassionate to themselves and others.

Psychologists Matthew Killingsworth and Daniel T. Gilbert found that almost half of the time we operate on "automatic pilot" or are unconscious of what we are doing or how we feel. Our mind wanders to somewhere else other than here and now. In addition to the constant mind-wandering, the various cognitive bias also affects our ability to have a more accurate understanding of ourselves.

RECOVERING FROM A SETBACK

#1 - Acknowledge your mistakes and take ownership.

#2 - Work to correct the perception of your brand.

#3 - Work with your mentor to discuss and develop a plan to improve.

#4 - Be resilient and move on; control what you can control and keep moving forward.

DEVELOPING YOUR PERSONAL BRAND

Identify your core values (honesty, integrity, beliefs), your passions, and your talents. Utilize Gallop Strengths Finders to determine strengths.

Start by answering the following questions:

How do you absorb, think about, and analyze information and situations?
How do you make things happen?
How do you influence others?
How do you build and nurture strong relationships?

Write your strengths down then add words that you think represent and describe your brand. Meet with mentors to determine your values and your brand. Look to friends and family to see what your do well. Ask them what you don't do well. Ask them what they think your brand is. Remember, if you find out your brand is not what you thought it was you can start working to change it.

However, be yourself. Sometimes as people begin developing their brand, they try to change themselves to fit into a brand that other people want. There may be things you need to change, but you need to be yourself because that will resonate with most folks. You want to separate yourself from everyone else; just don't be something you are not. Just being yourself is being genuine and sincere to others.

Take an Interest in Others. When you take an interest in others and care about them, you will be amazed what people will think about you. They will picture a good brand for you because you are putting their interests in front of your own interests

CORE ELEMENTS OF SUCCESSFUL PERSONAL BRANDING

It really struck me how personal branding is so valuable to employees, yet it does not appear that employees get training on what peers, customers, and leadership think your brand is and how to develop and possibly change your brand. So, here are the following attributes I have seen in the "best of the best."

Humble, learner, interpersonal skills, smart, and hungry: You don't have to have all these elements, but to be humble, want to learn, communicate well, and being a hard worker will give you a heck of a brand.

Positive attitude and high energy: Staying positive, having a great attitude, living the dream with high energy and passion are very positive branding attributes.

Perfect your storytelling stories and skills: Tell your brand story to everyone. We all have stories that will give insight to who we are. For example, one of our sales reps was a professional soccer player. What a story this rep could to tell everyone to continue the development of his brand.

Cultivate strong work relationships (trust, respect, empathy, integrity, accountability, and competence): Building those relationships leads to a great brand. People will like you, want to follow you, and be mentored by you.

How do you balance humility with personal branding being driven to move forward?

You need to maintain the highest degree of humility and still move forward with success. Personal branding requires increasing confidence. Humility requires a focus on serving others while not being self-serving and self-centered. Many things are out of your control; that is why you have to maintain and sustain the right pathway of confidence balanced with humility.

Here is a great story about how companies look at their employees; "It is what it is." Here are how most company leaders look at personal branding or define Personal Branding for any person. Let's say a person is made up of a pie chart; 100% is the starting point. Most companies, if not all, view most people are 95% good, i.e. they work hard, do a good job, have good skills for their position, and want to do what's right. So now the remaining 5% of the pie chart is considered the mistakes they have made in their career (real or perceived), and the weaknesses of that person.

You are probably going to be the optimistic group that believes that companies look at the 95% good in that employee, and give them raises, promotions, rewards, and "pats on the back."

Unfortunately, most companies spend more time analyzing the 5% of the employee that made or will make some mistakes and has weaknesses or flaws.

We need to look more at the 95% of people and keep developing their strengths to be the best of the best. We need to look less on wanting them to fix their weaknesses. For some reason, that is easier said than done.

That is where humility steps in on your balance chart. Choose to put those people with 95% good in positions with all those strengths they have; instead of penalizing them with 5% not so good. Don't get me wrong, as a leader or colleague, you want to know what someone's mistakes or weaknesses are; that way you can help them improve and put them into positions where they can use their strengths to the fullest.

Personal branding humbly and confidently emphasizes your strengths and builds on them while still improving and minimizing weaknesses. Find that balance for you and keep growing from the 95% good to 96%...and beyond!

DEVELOPING YOUR PERSONAL BRANDING

I went to VIED (Value in Employee Development), a really engaging course on personal branding and tools to develop your employees. One of the things this brought up was if you don't develop your own brand, others will do it for you, and you may not like what they think of you. That is why it is critical to begin developing your brand now. Developing your brand will allow you to align with your boss' perception of you. Check in frequently with colleagues, friends, and other executives to make sure your brand is doing okay.

The Gallup Organization came up with thirty-four distinct "talent themes" that best describe the range of human uniqueness observed during their research:

1. Achiever – one with a constant drive for accomplishing tasks

2. Activator – one who acts to start things in motion

3. Adaptability – one who is especially adept at accommodating to changes in direction/plan

4. Analytical – one who requires data and/or proof to make sense of their circumstances

5. Arranger – one who enjoys orchestrating many tasks and variables to a successful outcome

6. Belief – one who strives to find some ultimate meaning behind everything they do

7. Command – one who steps up to positions of leadership without fear of confrontation

8. **Communication – one who uses words to inspire action and education**

9. Competition – one who thrives on comparison and competition to be successful

10. Connectedness – one who seeks to unite others through commonality

11. **Consistency – one who believes in treating everyone the same to avoid unfair advantage**

12. Context – one who is able to use the past to make better decisions in the present

13. Deliberative – one who proceeds with caution, seeking to always have a plan and know all of the details

14. Developer – one who sees the untapped potential in others

15. Discipline – one who seeks to make sense of the world by imposition of order

16. **Empathy – one who is especially in tune with the emotions of others**

17. Focus – one who requires a clear sense of direction to be successful

18. Futuristic – one who has a keen sense of using an eye towards the future to drive today's success

19. Harmony – one who seeks to avoid conflict and achieve success through consensus

20. Ideation – one who is adept at seeing underlying concepts that unite disparate ideas

21. **Includer – one who instinctively works to include everyone**

22. Individualization – one who draws upon the uniqueness of individuals to create successful teams

23. Input – one who is constantly collecting information or objects for future use

24. Intellection – one who enjoys thinking and thought-provoking conversation often for its own sake, and also can data compress complex concepts into simplified models

25. Learner – one who must constantly be challenged and learning new things to feel successful

26. Maximizer – one who seeks to take people and projects from great to excellent

27. Positivity – one who has a knack for bringing the light-side to any situation

28. Relator – one who is most comfortable with fewer, deeper relationships

29. Responsibility – one who must follow through on commitments

30. Restorative – one who thrives on solving difficult problems

31. Self-Assurance – one who stays true to their beliefs, judgments and is confident of his/her ability

32. Significance – one who seeks to be seen as significant by others

33. Strategic – one who is able to see a clear direction through the complexity of a situation

34. **Woo – one who is able to easily persuade (short for "Winning Others Over")**

The Gallup group has developed an online test that will reveal the test-taker's top five themes. The "Clifton Strengths Finder" www.strengthsfinder.com is a web-based questionnaire, which will be able to define your individual "strengths." I strongly recommend you take the test; just remember Gallop Group only reveals your Top 5 strengths. It does not mean that you still don't have one of the 31 other strengths noted above. So, don't get depressed if, for example (like me), that "Strategic" does not show up. Just means you can be strategic; it just is not in the top five.

For those who are dying to know what my top strengths are, I highlighted them above. Enjoy, I had to come to the realization these are just my strengths; nothing more nothing less.

Chapter 5

Choose the Right Company

Determine what **values you are looking for in a company** like integrity, fairness, ethical, treat you like adults, and family driven. Speak to other company employees as well as customers to see how they view the company. No one has a more honest true opinion of a company than the customers. Through conversations with customers and employees, you will find out how ethical, fair, and especially how the company treats the customers and their employees. It may be the most critical assessment you make to determine if your values align with the company's core values.

Private versus Public. It is important to do your homework on any company that you want to interview with. Are they a publicly or privately traded company? Publicly traded companies worry about the quarterly results, they have shareholders to please, and most of the decisions are money driven. Publicly traded companies which are bought up and sold time and time again have a lot higher commission driven structure. They do not usually care about their people. You are a number. Trying to speak to the executives and president is almost impossible. They only worry about the quarterly earnings. They lay off a lot of people in the publicly traded environment. Many publicly owned companies give the appearance they portray values that align with what you are looking for, but their perceived degree of integrity may be in question.

Specific to the privately-owned company I work for, our decisions are made with the patient in mind and not the almighty dollar. The employees do not feel like a number and are able to speak to many of the executives including the president. Usually, privately owned companies don't make decisions based solely on money. We have not had a layoff in fifty-four plus years, and even when we are going through a transformation with our company, every employee has a position where most public companies would lay off people.

I probably would not have stayed with the same company for thirty-two years if I was not working with a privately-owned company.

You want a company that wants you to work with them; not for them. That means that they look at you as a team member; titles should not be important, and everyone should be willing to chip in and do any of the jobs. If it is a more "We" versus "I" attitude, then you know you're hanging around people with humility.

Company compensation and bonuses are important, but they are not a true incentive to measure your success. What I am saying is if you work for money as your highest measurement, you may not reach your career expectations. But if you work for the love of what you do, the money will come, and I guarantee you will reach your career expectations.

Many interviewers will provide false expectations with projections on bonuses, and how soon you can make six figures. I have never promised a candidate how soon they would reach $100,000 and beyond. I say, "You can make money; I just don't know how long it will take to get there."

You need to find your passion or love for what you do. Obviously when you start a job for the first time, it may be hard to have a passion or love going into the job. However, you can gain a pretty good understanding of the company, its integrity, and if you really like/love what they are asking you to sell. I personally got involved in medical sales because I wanted to sell something that I believed in, and more importantly help mankind! I could not have sold widgets, that if you had an extra buck, you would buy it from me. I had to sell something that could impact lives which kept me focused on the patient and not on money.

Do your research on the company's industry; what is their market share, and how are they viewed in the industry. Have as one of your list of questions to ask during the interview is: "Can you tell me what is in the pipeline for the next five years?"

Find out who your manager or "Direct Report" is going to be because with the right boss, you will have fun and walk around the office all the time with a smile on your face. Statistics indicate the biggest reasons folks leave a company is because of their boss. You will have a chance during interviews to speak directly to your boss. I would suggest you ask the following specific questions to help you understand how you will be managed.

- *How would you describe your management style?*
- *How do you want to be contacted, i.e. phone, text, e-mail, etc?*
- *Have them spell out their expectations for you.*

- *What is your leadership philosophy on development of employees? It is critical to have a leader/manager that wants to help you get you to where you want to go.*

- *Intuition: Use your gut as it will give you the final okay about the person.*

You just must keep an open mind, but don't wait years to move to another position in your company or leave if you find yourself walking on eggshells around your manager.

Preparation for Different Types of Interviews

Sales Scenarios:

a. *Selling Exercise* – I select some object on my desk and ask the interviewee to sell it to me. I will go out of the room for 5 minutes, then return and let them sell the object to me.

To prepare for this selling exercise, practice a two-to-three-minute selling presentation. Imagine the person is sitting across from you is a good friend and you are just having conversation over coffee. You will have a much more successful outcome.

b. *Writing Exercise* – I will ask them to write an e-mail to a prospective client. I am using this writing exercise to see if they have good writing skills and good use of grammar.

One of the most profound stories around interviewing that I have heard is from Bruce Gingles, one of my mentors. In the middle of the interview, he would get up out of his chair, give them a business card with a doctor's information, and have them write an introductory letter to a physician on his computer. He wanted to see the creativity in the letter and if it was compelling enough to get the doctor to agree to a meeting.

Bruce would leave the room and give them around 30 minutes to write the e-mail. He wanted to look at the grammar, sentence structure, and determine their writing ability. He also was one to stress the importance of cover letters. He would tell them that if there had been even one grammatical mistake on their cover letter, they wouldn't have gotten an interview with him.

THE CUSTOMER SLAM DUNK

Many years ago, I was a sales rep for our Critical Care Unit in Florida. I was in the territory for several years, when I was offered an opportunity to move over to our Surgery Unit as a Product Manager. I worked with a tremendous person, friend, and professional partner, Dave Paulus. He was an anesthesiologist at the University of Florida in Gainesville, Florida, and we had built up a tremendous relationship with him. His hospital was the #1 account in the country. Dave was not happy when I was no longer his rep, so he called my mentor, friend, and boss, Bruce Gingles. He asked Bruce to put me back into the sales position, so I could continue to be his rep. Bruce came up with the ingenious idea to have Dave interview our final candidate for this sales position. What better way to get one of our top customers to sign off on our hiring this person. I heard Dave Paulus was a tough interviewer and asked questions like, "If I called you at 3:00 p.m., how quickly will you return my call?" Another question was, "If I needed a product for a case, can you get it to me by tomorrow morning?"

Companies pay the reps, but the reps really work for the customers. Thank you, Bruce, for a brilliant interview method to find the right person. I call it "Customer Slam dunk."

- c. *Dinner Interviews* – I will take my final two candidates to dinner to observe how they act in a social environment. I look for humble, hungry, smart, learner, and interpersonal skills. My advice to those being interviewed: Do not drink. Listen, engage, and be self-aware.

- d. *Feedback* – I seek feedback from the taxi driver who brought the person from the airport to the interview. I also get feedback from other employees; especially the admin folks like the person at front desk or the person who gave them a tour of the facility.

It is important once the interviewee sets foot in the taxi or a company car to head to their interview, they are always very self-aware of their surroundings. Until they are back in the airport, they do not know which person will see or hear something they say or do that will provide feedback that could jeopardize their opportunity. I have seen candidates not get the job because of their "rude comments" to the admin folks or even to the travel agent who booked their flight for the interview.

A red flag is when the candidate does not treat the "front desk person" or the person who takes them around on a tour with respect. "Watch your P's and Q's."

Write thank you notes, use creativity, dress appropriately, shake hands. "Handwritten" "thank you" letters are critical to a successful interview; especially if you want to receive the job. The letters need to be prepared before you come to the interview and left at the front desk before you leave. Follow up with an e-mail before you leave the airport to go home. I have seen where some hiring managers won't even hire the person if they don't receive a thank you e-mail with 24 hours (they really expect it sooner).

You need to be professionally dressed. You can never over dress for an interview. Use a nice firm handshake with everyone you meet and look everyone in the eyes.

> Think "humble and kind" the entire time you speak to anyone in the company.

What is the necessary prep work before an interview?

Do your homework on the company. Know the company inside and out before you walk into the interview. Use my "Less is More" Chipism. I would much rather sit across from you and hear a few things that you know really well about my company versus a lot of mumble jumble rambling where you do not get all your facts straight. Prepare by calling folks who work at the company, use the internet, and call customers. Spend time on the Company website. No excuse not to know something about the company. Get the facts straight!

Do your homework on the widget. Understand the "widget" that the company wants you to sell. It's amazing the people that do not understand the widget when they come to the interview. The worst thing I have ever heard, could hear, and should hear is, "I love your product." That means they don't know anything. "Oh, your product is great. Oh, your product is fantastic." It tells me the candidate is not prepared for this interview. They do not even know the name of our "best product" or the features and benefits of our product. It just infuriates me that folks come to interviews not prepared more often than "you can shake a stick at." Make sure you know the company and the product they want you to sell before you go through that door!

I get asked the question all the time, "How can I knock it out of the park in an interview?" I am like a broken record when I say, "Preparation, Preparation, Preparation, know the company, and know the widget. Use the Chipism, "less is more" and what you do know, know it very, very well.

Don't Let the Resumé Speak for You

Too many candidates are driven by their resumé. They feel that their resumé sells them and that is wrong. It is emphatically wrong. They do not think they have to spend the time researching and doing their homework They are letting their resumé speak for them. I am not saying the resumé is not important, but it is just a small part of the interview.

However, a resumé must contain what I call "The Must See."

- One page
- Cover page, short and sweet, very succinct
- No grammatical mistakes in resumé and cover letter
- Chronologic order in years of your different employments (no gaps, or be ready to explain)
- Don't stretch the truth; put accurate GPA and degrees

Chip's Tips for a Successful Phone Interview

Remember that phone interviews are to weed candidates out and find the right ones to move forward with an "in person" interview. I advise using the K.I.S.S. method – "Keep It Simple Stupid."

The first thing is to start learning phone skills and here are some tips and a process to follow:

Work on your phone conversation. Call a friend or two and practice talking to them like you are being interviewed. They can play the part of the employer.

Be yourself, smile, have a good tone in your voice, and be excited. They want to hear the passion in your voice. Speak to them with the same facial expressions, smile, and tone in your voice you would use when meeting them in person. Your passion, your tone, and your smile will resonate to the person through the phone. They want to hear that you are excited to receive their phone call and to talk and to communicate with them.

Picture the person sitting across from you like you are having a conversation with your best friend over coffee. This is important because you will be relaxed and act more like yourself on the phone. Most people tend to be low key, almost too reserved and quiet on the phone. Imagine yourself in a comfortable, peaceful mental zone and you will do well on your phone interview.

Make some notes prior to the call. Have 4-5 questions to ask during the phone interview. It shows your interest in the company. It shows you are driven, you want to learn more about the company, the industry, and the position. Having prepared questions will show confidence.

You need to speak and pronounce your words clearly. Many people mumble on the phone, and if I can't hear you and understand you, I am not going to hire you.

Be aware of what the interviewer is looking for from you on the phone. They are going to ask some of the following questions:

What are your hobbies and interests outside of work?
Are you involved in community service?
Why do you want this job?
What drives you to be successful?

As an interviewer, I will say, "It does not sound like you really want this job." I want to see how they respond! I want to hear their excitement and passion about this opportunity. I also want to see if there is a mutual admiration, a mutual respect, and a mutual interest. Both of us need to get off the phone, excited about each other. It is a two-way phone interview. It is like "dating." We are just getting to know each other and all we have is this phone interview to decide if we want to meet and possibly work together.

Fine Tune Your Phone Skills

Prepare, Prepare, Prepare. You must prepare more for a phone interview than an "in person interview" since they can't see you, they can't get deep inside you.

Prepare some good questions/ comments/ responses.

- Know the job description of what you are interviewing for.

- Tell them what you are currently doing.

- Ask for the information you need to know.

- Know the company and the widget.
- Verify your salary expectations.

I know a phone interview is like "speed dating," but financial discussions need to be vetted. I have seen candidates come into face-to-face interviews and find out that the salary is far off what both expect. The conversation can end quickly during an interview if everyone is not on the same page regarding salaries.

SETTING UP MEETINGS/ APPOINTMENTS

Many of the same skills are needed to set up meetings and appointments with your customers as a phone interview for employment.

ENERGY
PASSION
ENTHUSIASM

You need to connect with and impress the customer, admin, secretary, or assistant who is on the other end of your phone conversation. **Preparation is very important.**

- *Research the customer prior to your call to find out what they do and their specialty.*
- *Use referrals to connect and get the appointments. Through your research you may find that other customers you work with know this customer.*
- *Before your call, see if you can find out the names of ancillary folks – people who answer the phone or who are in office. The*

- *way to do it is to call them to ask those questions to find out about their office folks and their policies.*

- *Any personal information you can get you can use to connect, break down the barriers, and try to start a personal relationship.*

- *Follow up with a thank you note. Try to deliver it in person the next day.*

- *Follow up with a call back to the customer, especially if they say the following, "I will check to see if he/she wants to set up a meeting." Make sure you call the person by their name. That will impress that person who really may not even remember you called a few days earlier.*

Even if you can't get an appointment from your call to set up meeting with a customer, get all pertinent information about your specific potential customer and the ancillary people, too. The phone interview is still a success if you have been able to obtain vital customer information.

INTERVIEWING 101

This chapter dealt with a variety of interview scenarios. As you can see, you will be involved in the interviewing process throughout your career. It begins with interviewing for a position whether it is a phone and/or a face-to-face interview. Your career in sales will involve interviews with customers throughout your time in field sales. You may even one day become the interviewer.

One thing should have become very clear as you read through this chapter, though. The most important part of every type of interview is your preparation.

What do you need to do to prepare for any job interview?

What do you need to do to prepare for a phone interview?

What do you need to do to prepare for a phone interview with a customer?

What do you need to do to prepare to conduct an interview?

Note: I have provided some interview worksheets and potential questions in the resource appendix at the end of the book to help you prepare for conducting an interview and can also help you prepare for an interview with a potential employer.

Chapter 6

Cultivate a Healthy Work/Life Balance

American journalist Paul Krassner observed that anthropologists define happiness as having as little separation as possible between your work and your play.[19]

Work/Life balance is one of the most critical components in being successful and happy in life. Work/Life balance is a concept including the proper prioritization between work (career and ambition) and lifestyle (health, pleasure, leisure, family).

I look at Work/Life balance like a bell curve:

Stage 1 is where you give 150 percent to your job, you have very little personal/ home life, and you need family, friends, or spouse/ partner to be there in heart, soul, mind, and body. That is the #1 key because **if you don't have stability, understanding, and a little humility on the home front, it won't work.**

The important message is you must dig deeply inside yourself and put your heart and soul into the new job for the first five to seven years to develop your brand, your knowledge, your skills, and your performance will be measured. Home/personal life will not suffer if everyone on your team is on board and understands your objectives and goals and feels part of this journey.

My Stage 1 started at the age of twenty-five. I was single and moved to Tampa, Florida as a sales rep for Cook Medical. I was scared to death. I moved to Florida with no friends or family there for support. I traveled a lot and spent all my time developing my territory. I married my wife Cyrilla, at the end of my Stage 1. She was a "rock" as I was traveling a lot and trying to move up the corporate ladder. She knew I had to travel to build my territory. She always said, "Go do what you need to do and I will be here when you come home." This first stage in your career won't work or sustain itself unless you have a strong family and support. You go get your business, knowing your family team will take care of everything while you are trying to build your career.

Stage 2 is where you may be getting your MBA or begin to consider other positions inside or outside your company. People are starting to talk about you around the water cooler, the executives are discussing you at their leadership meetings, your customers like you, and your performance speaks for itself. Home/personal life is starting to come into balance more frequently because you are beginning to be a confident, seasoned, knowledgeable employee, and you can do your job more over the phone, email and text. You have built up a trust with your customers. You are able to juggle work and some home priorities better and able to schedule some personal commitments around work.

Stage 2 happened to me during the same time I was getting my MBA. I had seven years under my belt when I met my wife in my MBA class. We married and then had three little kids as I was trying to finish my MBA and continue to build my work portfolio. She had to take care of a lot of things, but I was far enough along in my job that I could make it home for kid events, and spend more quality time, like birthdays, and special events. My wife understood this stage of my career was heading towards my own professional development and hopefully obtaining a leadership position.

If it was not for my wife, I'm not sure I would have survived Stage 2. She continued to carry most of the load at home. I was at peace working knowing "Home was fine." Not worrying about any problems at home took a load of me while I was trying to make my territory #1 in the country.

Stage 3 is generally 15-25 years in your career. Probably the best years for good Work/Life balance! Secure in your position/brand at the company, you are able to schedule work around important personal time and commitments. You can be home for the kids and their special events like when their school has a "doughnuts and dad's" event, you can go and when it is over, then you can head back to work.

It is really a great time in life because you and your career are still growing and you are secure enough in your skin and your job, that home becomes the priority. Work for the most part is scheduled around your home life. Work is still the driving force, but you have built up a steady business and you have learned to be able to secure business from a distance. You don't have to be there in person. It is a fun time because finally all your hard work is paying off.

Stage 4 is the Empty-Nester Stage. The kids are gone, you and your spouse have time to talk to each other and have more time to travel. People are living longer, therefore, working longer. "The Empty Nester Stage" is great because it allows you to start a new position and can travel as needed. Stage 4 of the "Work/Life Balance" could be the best stage of all. You have taken care of your kids and now you can take care of you and your spouse. My wife and I are now

"Empty Nesters" and I am starting a new position with a lot of travel. Many times, she can travel with me now.

A Note from My Wife

Chip is definitely Type A but a tremendous part of his character is being a devoted family man. There have definitely been times in our 26 years of marriage when he has needed a little nudge in balancing work and family life. Very early in our marriage my mother-in-law witnessed a disagreement we were having. She invited me to lunch and an afternoon of shopping and gave me a little advice – if you want Chip to do something it is best to plant the seed and let the idea become his. Once the idea becomes his then he will take charge and make it happen. She was spot on with her advice.

Type A's definitely like to steamroll, but as the spouse you can't be afraid to push back in order to keep them grounded to family. When the kids were really little it was super hard with his travel. He would come home exhausted from his trip, but I was also tired. Fortunately, Chip loves being a part of his kids' lives so he'd jump in and help with baths and story time!

I also believe that you have to pick your battles. Some aren't worth fighting and some you know you can never win. You also must be understanding and realize that there are times when the job will come first and that he can't always be there. You have to work really hard at communicating and synchronizing the family calendar with the work calendar. One of my nonnegotiable rules was always family dinners and family game nights. I believe that those simple times together were critical to uniting our family and keeping our marriage healthy. A final tip is when playing euchre, it is best if Chip and I aren't partners!

Here's my "Take Home" Message for you. Work/Life is an important balance to be successful and happy. Work/Life goes through stages of building your career through hard work until you finally hit the stage where you're stable, secure, and good at what you do. You can actually work around the home life events with the family versus trying to schedule home life events around work. Experience allows you to work smarter, not longer, so when you get to Stage 4 someday, it will be fun.

Good Home Balance Means:

- **Get Support**. There is an African proverb that says it best: "It takes a Village to raise a family." Chatting with friends and family can be important to your success at home, at work, and can even improve your health. I use my friends and family to download my stress issues, my concerns, and share my successes.

- **Unplug**. You must "unplug" and turn off the phone or put it somewhere in your home where you really can't see it. "Out of sight, Out of Mind." You need time to turn off all the stuff in your head like what you did not get done that day, and what you are going to get done tomorrow.

- **Stay Active**. Aside from its well-known physical benefits, regular exercise reduces stress, depression, and anxiety, and enables people to better cope with adversity. Make time in your schedule for the gym or to take a walk after work. My wife and I walk the dog together. It gives us exercise as well as time to catch up about what is going on in our lives and our kids' lives.

- **Take Care of the Family**. When you get home each evening, it is all about family. Family comes first, especially in helping at home, whether it is catching up, helping with dinner, or doing the dishes.

Good Work Balance

- **Right Expectations for Daily Goals**. Being able to meet priorities helps us feel a sense of accomplishment and control. So, be realistic about workloads and deadlines. Make a "To do" list and take care of important tasks first and eliminate unessential ones. When I know my week is particularly packed with calls and meetings, I find it incredibly beneficial to take 30 minutes on Sunday to think about what my top priorities are and get organized for the week ahead of me. It's never fun to think about work on a Sunday, but it pays off when I wake up and already have a game plan to tackle on Monday morning.

- **Be Time Efficient.** Work smart, not longer. "Busy does not mean Productive."

- **Ask for Flexibility**. Flex time and telecommuting are quickly becoming established as necessities in today's business world. Many companies are drafting work/life policies. If you ask, they might allow you to work flexible hours or from home a day a week.

- **Take Breaks Throughout the Day**. Taking a break at work isn't only acceptable, it's often encouraged by many employers. Small breaks at work or on any project will help clear your head and improve your ability to deal with stress and make good decisions when you jump back into the grind. Don't feel guilty about taking breaks. If you find yourself staying at work past 6 p.m., take small breaks throughout the day to break things up and focus on non-work things. I have started taking longer breaks that I have penciled in my calendar during the day to go walk.

Whatever you need to do to get yourself to rejuvenate, just do it!

When you are fit and trim, you are going to look at things positively. Exercising daily relieves stress and you feel good about yourself. Others will usually begin to make comments to how good you look. That really pumps you up and you feel like a million dollars! You will have a more positive outlook and you feel better about yourself.

My Story

I obviously believe you must have a healthy Work/Life Balance. I am better today than I was fifteen years ago. I have discovered if we are going to be good at what we do in the sales industry, we can't always turn it off at 5:00 p.m. on a Friday afternoon and wait to resume business on Monday. What we can do is learn to put things in perspective according to priorities and importance. That way we know what e-mails or conversations we need to respond to, so we make sure we balance our personal life and family. I have had to go through that process of learning how to be better at home. What is interesting about this is if we have a passion for something, we are going to figure out how to balance both, so we can take care of our customers and take care of our family.

If you love what you do, you will figure it out. Like when I am on vacation and I'm on the 18th hole, about ready to pull out my driver and I get a phone call. I know if it is from an important customer or not. I believe I can enjoy my golf game and still take care of customers if I do it the right way. Sometimes it boils down to whether you have provided the right expectations to those customers. Figure out what is right for you, your career, and your family and make it work.

Work/Life Balance

When it comes to making sure you have great support at home, I can't stress enough how important my wife, Cyrilla, has been. I would not be the person I am today without her selfless support. She has been my best friend, my sounding board, and my therapist—listening to my frustrations, my concerns, and my ideas. My mother taught me a golden rule: "Marry someone that is brighter than you." I sure did!

The biggest thing I have learned is that I am a winner because I have a great family and great friends.

Remember this Chipism: "When the good Lord calls you upstairs, it is not going to matter what you did for a living; it is just going to matter whether you were a good person and were you good to your family!"

A Final Word

Keep Growing!

About five years ago, I received some comments from some of my customers about my career path that got me thinking. You can't imagine how it made me feel when my customer asked, "Why aren't you the president of Cook Medical yet?" Then another long-time customer said, "I bet you run the show now. You are the face of Cook Medical." It made me feel like I had hit the pinnacle of success. Even with such glowing endorsements from my customers, I could not control where I was on my career path.

I think I was feeling a little stagnant in my career, plus I wanted to continue developing my brand. I didn't feel I was growing professionally. So, I took it upon myself to look for other ways to grow.

I started teaching and sharing my sales experiences at colleges with students. I wanted to personally and professionally grow. Teaching and sharing ended up being a passion of mine. I really have enjoyed spending time with the students and being totally honest and transparent.

Another area of personal growth for me that happened as I was teaching was a desire to write down what I was teaching. A number of people had asked me to write a book. As I prepared my material for the book, I discovered enough to ultimately write two books. As both books neared completion, I began to let a few people know that I was nearing the end, and I had two books coming out very soon.

People reacted to my announcement in different ways, and some were humorous. The first response was like this: "**You**," with a pointed finger, "writing books!?" Their tone was one of complete disbelief.

The second response was, "Wow, not bad." They sounded surprised and a little awed. Finally, in others, I saw a shift, a change in their entire perception of me. It went up! Now, perception is reality. Having a book published seemed to give me, in their eyes, more credibility, gravitas, and credentials. Now, that's very cool.

"Chipisms" were born in teaching and then included throughout my books; right there in the classroom my perception started changing when I saw the students focused on my every subtle point and my life lessons. My "Chipisms" are really meant to be said or delivered when I want you to put it to memory, and live day by day trying to implement something in your life both personally and professionally. Don't leave this book just yet as I will leave you at the end with a brief resource page on my top "Chipisms" to guarantee you success in "Life and Career."

Too many people want to blame the company for their unhappiness when all they have to do is seek ways to grow professionally. I sincerely hope this book has helped you see you have some options to grow your professional career through humility and have fun doing it.

Appendix 1

Resources You Really Need!

INTERVIEW WORKSHEETS AND SUGGESTED QUESTIONS

Interpersonal – (Intelligent, People Smart, Relational, Exec Test, Reliable, Critical Thinking, Adaptable)

1. Have you ever worked with a difficult colleague or boss? How did you respond to the situation?

    a. *Insight:* By asking the candidate about a difficult work relationship, you will learn if he or she can read situations and people and handle them skillfully.

2. What roles have you been able to learn quickly?

    a. *Insight:* You want to see if the person has technical skills like working with various business software. Also see if they pick up things quickly and is a quick learner.

3. How would you describe your personality?

    a. *Insight:* Look for how accurately the person describes what you are observing and how introspective he or she is. Smart people generally know themselves and find it interesting to talk about their behavioral strengths and weaknesses. People who seem stumped or surprised by this question might not be terribly smart when it comes to people.

4. What would coworkers say about you that would be annoying?

    a. *Insight:* Everyone annoys someone, sometimes. Especially at home. Smart people are not immune to this. But neither are they in the dark about it and they tend to moderate these behaviors at work.

5. Give an example of how you've demonstrated empathy to a teammate.

    a. *Insight:* The issue is whether the candidate seems to understand what others are feeling. Now, there are certain personality types that are less empathic than others and that's fine. What you're looking for here is an indication that the person values empathy and whether he or she has an understanding of his or her own strengths or weaknesses in this area.

6. What have you done to deal with an irate customer?

    a. *Insight*: See how the person describes the situation; did they turn a negative into a positive.

7. Give me an example of a time you successfully communicated with a person who disliked you.

    a. *Insight*: Not everyone is going to like you no matter how hard you try. Observe if the person still treats the person with respect knowing the person did not like them.

8. Discuss a time when your integrity was challenged.

    a. *Insight*: Do they have a story where a customer or employee wanted you to bend the rules; what did you say or do about it?

9. Describe a situation where others you were working with on a project disagreed with your ideas.

    a. *Insight*: Ask, How did you handle other people disagreeing with you…with humility or were you vengeful?

10. Describe a time when your company dropped the ball and how you dealt with people involved.

    a. *Insight*: Find out if the person took ownership knowing "they are the company," or did they blame the company.

This is really a telltale sign not to hire that person if they blame the company; they will always blame the company if things go wrong.

11. Describe how you handle change. Provide an example where you've experienced significant change and how you reacted.

    a. *Insight*: Find out if the person reacted positively or negatively to change — will tell you a lot about the person.

DETERMINED — (HUNGRY, ENERGY, ADAPTABLE, EXECUTION, PERSEVERANCE, WORK ETHIC)

1. Tell me what kind of hours you generally work. How does that differentiate from your peers?

    a. *Insight*: Hardworking people usually don't want to work nine to five unless their unique life situations demand it. If they do, they are usually getting additional work done at home. That's not to say that some people aren't stuck in dead-end, nine to five jobs and are itching to get out and do something challenging. But if a candidate is satisfied with a predictable schedule and talks too much about "balance," there's a chance he or she isn't terribly hungry. Again, not a litmus test, but a red flag. None of this is to advocate that people should prioritize their work over their families. Not at all. It's just that when a candidate focuses a lot on the hours that they're expected to work, they may not be the kind of hungry team player you need.

2. Tell me about a time you set difficult goals. What did you do to achieve them? Walk me through the process and purpose.

    a. *Insight*: Does the person describe a plan to achieve the goals; want to hear the steps of the plan. Does not matter as much if they achieved them; more important that they tried a well thought out plan

3. Tell me about a time your company did not deliver on product/service and how you responded/handled it.

    a. *Insight*: Hope you stood up for the company in front of customer, and in private it bothered you. That is okay!

4. Provide a scenario how you've overcome a challenge in your current role. What did you do?

    a. *Insight*: I love to hear stories about overcoming the challenge — want to know the challenge and how did they react to the challenge.

5. Tell me about a time when you worked with a colleague who was not doing their share of work. How did you handle it?

a. *Insight*: It is good to see if the person will be honest with the other person and share their concerns with kindness.

6. Tell me about a time you have inherited a customer. What steps did you take to establish a rapport with them? What did you do to gain their trust?

    a. *Insight*: Inherited or not inherited? It should not change how a candidate builds a relationship, and treats them like they want to be treated.

7. What are your short-term goals? Long-term goals?

    a. *Insight*: Want to see if person thinks "big picture," and also do they have enough drive to have goals; short and long. Tells a lot about a person who has goals in their life. We want those types of people in any organization.

HUMBLE – (HUMILITY, INTEGRITY, BEER TEST, EXEC TEST, RELIABLE)

1. Describe a situation with a customer where you made a mistake. How did you handle it?

    a. *Insight*: Do they take ownership and admit the mistake immediately?

2. Tell me about your biggest career accomplishment to date.

    a. *Insight*: Look for more mentions of we than I. Of course, it isn't about being so simplistic as to count the responses. In the event that someone refers to himself or herself individually more than as a member of a team, probe for whether he or she was working alone or with others.

3. Tell me about your weaknesses and how you overcome them.

a. *Insight*: Look for admittance of weaknesses and shortcomings, nothing wrong with recognizing them.

4. What role do you typically play in a team?

   a. *Insight*: Does the person's behavior reveal whether they are a leader or follower; whether they serve others or seek to take control of the team.

5. If you found a $50 bill what would you do with it?

   a. *Insight*: True integrity, honesty, or lack of it will show its head in their response.

6. Describe a time when you had to stand up and support someone else.

   a. *Insight*: Do they stand up for others and put other's needs in front of their own.

7. Did you ever work for someone where you didn't agree with their values/how they won business? How did you handle your work relationship with this person?

   a. *Insight*: Now you are going to really see the honesty and integrity of the person. Remember to always do the right thing, and honesty is always the best policy.

8. Have you ever had someone take credit for work you did? How did you react to that?

   a. *Insight*: Can the person turn the other cheek, and do they understand that two wrongs do not make a right? Does not do any good to call them out, especially if they are your boss or can impact you at work.

9. Tell me about a time you felt passionate about getting something done, but your manager didn't support you. How did you react?

    a. *Insight*: Does the person show empathy for his/her manager and didn't throw the DR under the bus? Also did the person go ahead and get the project done despite their manager. That would tell me a lot if they did!

10. Tell me about a business decision you made that you ultimately regretted. What happened?

    a. *Insight*: Did the candidate take complete ownership around their business decision that they regretted. See if the candidate says they made a mistake and is truly sorry.

11. Who was the last person you fell out with? What happened?

    a. *Insight*: It is interesting to find this out, not so much "who the person is they fell out with" as much as to see them show class in discussing the situation, and did they or did they not throw the person under the bus.

12. Describe your current team. What do you like/dislike?

    a. *Insight*: By asking a team related question, it may be apparent if he or she values a team effort and is willing to do what is necessary for the good of the team. Encourage the candidate to describe specific interactions with colleagues and experiences working on a team.

13. What is your most embarrassing moment of your career? Or biggest failure?

a. *Insight*: Look for whether the candidate celebrates that embarrassment or is mortified by it. Humble people generally aren't afraid to tell their unflattering stories because they're comfortable with being imperfect. Also, look for specifics and real references to the candidate's own culpability.

14. How do you handle apologies? To accept/give them.

    a. *Insight*: Look for and ask for specifics. Humble people are not afraid to say they are sorry, and they accept other people's genuine apologies with grace. People who do this usually have specific stories.

15. Can you tell me about someone who is better than you in an area that really matters to you?

    a. *Insight*: Look for the candidate to demonstrate a genuine appreciation for others who have more skill or talent. Humble people are comfortable with this. Ego-driven people often are not.

Learner – (Hungry, Learner, Intelligent, Critical Thinker)

1. Describe a situation to solve a difficult problem. What did you do?

    a. *Insight*: Steps to study a problem before making a decision.

2. *(After clinical presentation)* Can you tell me a little more about X vs. Y

    a. Insight: It will tell if they really know what they presented; some people don't understand really what they present;

just words they use without knowing their meaning or having experienced their impact.

3. Tell me about a time when you've solved a problem in a unique/unusual way. What was the outcome?

   a. *Insight*: Describe the problem and what was the unusual way you resolved it. Looking more for how they tried to resolve it knowing that one does not always get the outcome one is seeking.

4. Have you ever had to make a decision without all the information? How did you handle it?

   a. *Insight*: Want to see if they accepted the outcome; especially if outcome from their decision was not good. Prepare to see if they blamed others because they did not have all the information. Pretty typical response from most people. Doesn't mean it is ever right to blame others

5. What is one of the most difficult decisions you have had to make at work. What was the result?

   a. *Insight*: Did they make the decision with humility, kindness, and thinking of others beside themselves? Then whatever happens, happens because you did it the right way.

6. Who/what are some outside sources that you have used to grow professionally?

   a. *Insight*: Hopefully get a feeling on their ambition, drive, and are they self-motivated to grow, get better, and keep improving. Are they a learner and want to grow?

7. What did you do to establish rapport with a customer you inherited?

   a. *Insight*: Do you sense or hear that they treated the customer the same or treated them differently because they inherited them?

8. What do you know of our products and the procedures we're involved in?

   a. *Insight*: Less is more; what they do know about our products and procedures, do they know it well?

9. Describe a situation you had to adjust to changes over which you had no control. How did you handle it?

   a. *Insight*: Did they move on and accept the changes or get frustrated or mad.

10. How do you manage highly complex/ever-changing information?

    a. *Insight*: You want to see how they handle their nerves, and does it change how they act and treat people and are they negative or complain about their work?

11. What do you do when you are not working?

    a. *Insight*: Look out for too many time-consuming hobbies that suggest the candidate sees the job as a means to do other things. That's not to say that there is one specific kind of activity that is an indicator of not being hungry. And it's certainly not to say that you're looking for someone who has no interests in life outside of work. A long list of hobbies like extreme skiing, sled dog racing, storm chasing, and shark hunting might just be a red flag when it comes to someone who is not going to put the needs of the team ahead of personal pursuits.

12. Tell me about a time when you've presented to a group with little/no preparation. How did you handle them?

    a. *Insight*: Can the person show patience and calmness with the group? Can they speak off the cuff and impromptu? Did they show confidence? Did they speak to just having a conversation with the group, and not a presentation?

Appendix 2

Rules of Engagement

- When you bring your boss in on a problem, you need to have a solution or two in your pocket.

- Never embarrass your boss in front of others; especially their peers.

- Always have your sensitive conversations where you may have disagreements with your boss behind closed doors and try to stay calm.

- Always try to solve many problems yourself before escalating the problem to your boss.

- Try to understand the boss' communication and decision-making style. Some bosses take forever to make decisions, some don't make them at all, and some make poor decisions.

Appendix 3

"Chipisms"

When I am speaking at various events, people often ask me how I came up with the term "Chipism." In a class one day while I was teaching at Ball State, I was in one of my excitable, passionate moods, and I kept feeling the students were mesmerized about some of my idiotic thoughts and comments. Out of the blue, I yelled out to them, I have a "Chipism" for you. When I would say something I wanted them to listen to and remember, I would call it a "Chipism."

Chipisms became part of who I am, part of my DNA. Not long ago, a student approached me whom I had not seen in two years, and the first thing out of his mouth was, "I remember some of your Chipisms." Hearing that was music to my ears. While I have referred to these Chipisms throughout both of my books and devoted a chapter in *Everyday Sales Wisdom for Your Life & Career*, I wanted to list them for you in this appendix as a final reminder that everyone is in sales!

"Less is more."

I guess the best way to explain "less is more" is to use it in an applicable situation like preparing for an interview. I always stress to know the company and the widget that they want you to sell. I prefer knowing a few facts about the company and widget really well, instead of trying to know everything which can lead to overwhelming the listener and even confusing both of you.

"Have a Conversation not a Presentation."

This is one of my favorite Chipisms because most people are taught at many courses to learn how to present but not how to have a conversation. I am not saying don't learn how to put together a presentation for a meeting; just don't present it. Too many people get up in front of people as "robots," and they want to just present to someone with a very monotone voice, lack of facial expressions, and too scripted. They are not being themselves.

Let's go back to putting together presentations. It is a great idea to put slides together for your presentation. Just use your slides as a backdrop, and simply have conversation with your audience.

"Never close the door on a customer."

Statistics show it takes at least 7-8 attempts before you see a customer. Frustration creeps into your head after the 3rd or 4th try, and you are ready to give up. Don't ever give up on any customer! I never cared what a customer bought from me on Monday or two Mondays from now, or a year from Monday. What really mattered to me was the customer buying from me years later.

"Do the right thing."

Kem Hawkins, Ex-CEO, Cook Medical taught me the golden rule of "Do the Right Thing," and in the medical profession, "Do right by the patient."

Every day, ask yourself, or better yet look yourself in the mirror and ask the question; "Am I doing the right thing?" Always be ethical and have the highest integrity; so if you do it with the right intent and the right heart, I believe you will do the right thing.

"Perception is reality."

One of the most frustrating Chipisms that I have seen in my thirty-two years; but unfortunately, it is true in the corporate world and in any professional setting, "Perception is Reality." Quite simply, if someone else (like a boss) believes you did something wrong, and you believe you did not do it, "**you did it.**"

"The glass is half full."

People ask me more than you think, what does "The Glass Half Full" mean? "Is the glass half empty or half full?" is a common expression to indicate that a particular situation could be a cause for optimism (half **full**) or pessimism (half **empty**)? Most statistics say that people who look at the glass half empty are pessimistic by nature. We need more positive people in this country; positivity breeds positivity, and negativity breeds negativity. I wear a "stay positive" band that was designed by a Butler University cancer patient back in 2014.

"Johnny on the spot."

"Do what you say you are going to do and do it when you say you are going to do it." If you live every day with by that creed, you will be very successful.

"Honest as the day is long."

If someone is "honest as the day is long," they are very honest, consistent, and reliable person. The implication seems to be that he or she is honest all the time.

"If you solve a customer's problem, you have them in your pocket."

Customers never forget you if you solve their problem; you literally have them in your pocket, and they will be loyal "until the cows come home."

"The sun will come up the next morning; The sun rises every morning."

A sunrise puts our troubles in perspective. No matter how dark your life seems right now, a sunrise is waiting on your personal horizon.

"Just get dressed and get out of bed."

Get up and get going every day. Nothing good will happen until you leave the house and go see customers. Self-motivation is key especially when you are out in the field in sales. If you are not self-motivated, you will not be successful in sales.

"Plan Your Work and Work Your Plan."

Put together a "To-do list from one to ten action items for each day. It can be as simple as putting it down on a piece of paper and keeping the list before you all day.

"Never Assume Anything."

As soon as you start assuming, you fall into the trap that you accept everything as truth without checking.

"It's all about people."

The people I have worked with over the years have impacted me personally as well as professionally. Many of my customers have developed into friendships, many of my colleagues are now close friends of mine today. The people you work and serve every day are "what makes the world go round and round."

"It Is A Game of Chess."

Well, average managers play checkers and great leaders play chess. In checkers all the pieces are uniform and move in the same way; they are interchangeable. You need to plan and coordinate their movements certainly, but they all move at the same pace on parallel paths. In chess though, each type of piece moves in a different way and you can't play if you don't know how each piece moves. More importantly, you will not win if you don't think carefully about how you move the pieces.

"Everyone Is in Sales."

There is myth out there that if you literally do not go into sales, then you are not in sales. No matter what you do in life, you are in sales. You sell 3 things; a widget, a concept, or yourself. Everyone has the same GPA, test scores, and technical ability. What separates you from anyone else in your career is "you."

"You Find Mentors; They Do Not Find You."

It is important to seek out a mentor or mentors early in life; high school or college is a good start to find yourself a mentor. You never know where and when you will run into your mentor. They do not show up on your doorstep. You have to find them through networking, luck, and putting your hand out to say *hello*.

Tips to Finding a mentor:

— Look to a family member or a friend or a teacher (you already know and trust).

— Be willing to meet people; put your hand out and say hello, introduce yourself to all people.

— Look for those mentor qualities I described above-biggest quality is, "Do they have your best interest at heart?"

One final note; you will know when you meet that right person! It will become obvious because they want to help you, guide you, and open doors for you.

"Don't Let the Door Hit You on the Way Out."

Over the years, I have used this term quite often, "Don't let the door hit you on the way out." Don't be a complainer and ruin it for everyone else!

"Customers Buy from People They Like."

Here is a quote from a friend of mine, "People do not buy from salespeople because they understand their products; they buy because they felt the salesperson understood their problems."

"Sales is not Rocket Science."

Keep It Simple Stupid (K.I.S.S.), is what I say to myself continually!

"What Have We Done for the Salesperson Today?"

As far as I am concerned, no one would have any position in a company if it were not for the sales people. "Without salespeople companies don't exist."

"Don't Make It Harder Than What It Is."

Sometimes we over analyze. Sometimes we over think. Sometimes we get too complicated. We simply need to communicate, listen well, and problem solve with people.

"Take A Deep Breath and Wait for 24 Hours."

This is probably one of the most impactful Chipisms that I have ever come across. Before you respond to a difficult e-mail or text, take a deep breath and wait twenty-four hours until you calm down. Respond quickly and you will probably do or say something you will later regret.

"Treat People Like You Want to Be Treated."

I think it's the #1 Golden Rule in business, and basically the way you want to work with or lead people.

"Do It in Your Sleep."

"Do it in your sleep" is a very, very impactful phrase. It's much like, practice makes perfect. This is very similar to another Chipism, "Repetition, Repetition, Repetition."

"To Be on Time is to be Early."

"To be on Time is to be Early" is a behavior that has to become part of who you are; both personally and professionally.

"Sales is all about Preparation and Repetition."

All throughout the book, you hear me saying it is all about "Preparation, Preparation, and Repetition, Repetition." In sales, you can't prepare enough when learning and having conversations with customers. You are only as good as your preparation; simple as that! One of John Wooden's, the legendary basketball coach, famous quotes is, "Failing to prepare is preparing to fail."

"It is not What you Say to People; it is How You Say It."

Before you write an e-mail, a text, make a phone call, or tweet someone, think about "it is not what you say(write) to people; it is how you say (write) it." Too many people put their emotions into their communications; speak/write with kindness, and think of the other person's feelings, not your own. This is the crux of being humble and influencing people with humility.

"Never had a job in my life."

I was fortunate that I fell in love with what I do; if that happens to you, you will never have job, too.

"Business is always personal."

Business must become "Personal" for you to have long term success. Make sense? How does business lead to personal relationship?

— Build a trusting, loyal relationship.

— Bring in some personal connections that may align with the customer.

— Take care of your customer!

"Think Long Term; but Don't Act Short Term."

Don't get caught up in the weeds! Don't sweat the small stuff.

"Do what you say you are going to do, and do it when you say you are going to do it."

Very simple and very powerful; if you promise something to the customer, follow up and fulfill the promise. If you don't make good on your promise, you will lose the customer and lose the business.

"The Buck Stops Here."

Look yourself in the mirror. Take complete ownership on your performance…good or bad.

About the Author

From a Dental School drop-out to a National Sales Manager of a multi-billion-dollar medical device company, Chip Helm has honed his sales skills from the ground up. With anecdotal examples from his successes and failures, Chip's stories will have you laughing while you learn. Chip knows how to develop and maintain long-term relationships to help drive sales success. If it is personal branding, practicing humility, or following-up and following-through, his practical advice is applicable to anyone at any stage in their career. His mentoring and leadership has helped thousands of students and colleagues over his last three decades in sales. Chip is a regular guest lecturer at business schools around Indiana, including Purdue, Ball State, Butler University, and Indiana University. He is also a certified coach and college lecturer. His loves are family, work, and his home in Northern Michigan.

Chip holds a BA in Biology from Indiana University and an MBA from the University of South Florida. Married for twenty-six years, Chip met his wife, Cyrilla, at USF while in the MBA program. They have three adult children all pursuing education and professions in health and medical disciplines. Chip has worked for Cook Medical for over thirty-two years.

> "No Matter the Career you have chosen,
> **YOU ARE IN SALES."**
> —**Chip Helm**

Connect with Chip Helm

For More Information About Chip Helm's books, resources, podcasts, and events go to:

www.chiphelm.com

Contact Chip Helm at:

ChipHelm16@gmail.com

Get a copy now of Chip's book:
Everyday Sales Wisdom for Your Life & Career

Endnotes

[1] www.goodreads.com.you-can-do-it.JohnMason
[2] https://guykawasaki.com/the_art_of_schm-2/
[3] https://tinyurl.com/y84lbq4p
[4] www.pinterest.com/pin/48906345931006938
[5] https://www.workitdaily.com/personal-brand/
[6] Lair, Daniel J.; Sullivan, Katie; Cheney, George (2005). "Marketization and the Recasting of the Professional Self." Management Communication Quarterly. 18 (3): 307–343. doi:10.1177/0893318904270744.
[7] https://www.fastcompany.com/28905/brand-called-you
[8] Daniel Goleman is an internationally known psychologist who lectures frequently to professional groups, business audiences, and on college campuses. As a science journalist Goleman reported on the brain and behavioral sciences for *The New York Times* for many years. His 1995 book, *Emotional Intelligence* was on *The New York Times* bestseller list.
[9] http://www.danielgilbert.com/KILLINGSWORTH%20&%20GILBERT%20(2010).pdf
[10] www.gallupstrengthcenter.com/Gallup/StrengthsFinder
[11] Team Development is Critical — Develop Your Team Starting Now solutions.gallup.com/Training/Employees
[12] https://en.wikipedia.org/wiki/Now,_Discover_Your_Strengths

www.ingramcontent.com/pod-product-compliance
Lightning Source LLC
Chambersburg PA
CBHW072148170526
45158CB00004BA/1547